Handy Mom's Guide
GRILLING

The Fast, Easy Way to *Smokin'* Meals!

Published by Cool Springs Press,
101 Forrest Crossing, Suite 100, Franklin, Tennessee 37064.

Library of Congress Cataloging-in-Publication Data

Mayhew, Catherine.
  Handy mom's guide : grilling, the fast, easy way to smokin' meals! / by Catherine Mayhew.
     p. cm.
  ISBN 978-1-59186-0376-2 (alk. paper)
  1. Broiling. 2. Barbecue cookery. 3. Quick and easy cookery. I. Title. II. Title: Grilling, the fast, easy way to smokin' meals.

  TX687.M39 2008
  641.5'55--dc22

2007039546

ISBN: 978-1-59186-376-2

First Printing 2008
Printed in China
10 9 8 7 6 5 4 3 2 1

Managing Editor: Cindy Kershner

Cover and Book Design: Bill Kersey, Kersey Graphics

Recipe Editor: Jan Keeling

Production: S. E. Anderson

Handy Mom's Guide

GRILLING

The Fast, Easy Way to *Smokin'* Meals!

CATHERINE MAYHEW

COOL SPRINGS PRESS

FRANKLIN ,TENNESSEE

Acknowledgements

When my parents were newly married, my mother, Kay, gave my father, Troy, a book called *The Complete Barbecue Book* by John and Marie Roberson. The book was meant to be from me, and she inscribed it: "To Daddy from Cathy, Father's Day, June 20, 1954." I was two years old.

The book was a celebration of grilling in the 1950s, and my father used it fastidiously, not only for the recipes but as a receptacle for now-faded newspaper clippings for dishes he wanted to try. I still have the book, and I think it's significant that even back in the day when only men grilled, *The Complete Barbecue Book* was co-authored by a woman.

I want to thank my dad for giving me a love of outdoor cooking and an adventurous palate.

My own amazing husband, Mark, and my wonderful son, Noah, do not share my father's love of the grill, but they are enthusiastic consumers of everything it produces. I want to thank them for being my chief tasters and best critics (and for going without fried food for an extended period of time—not easy to do in the South!).

I'd also like to thank my editor, Cindy Kershner, who made this a better book with her enthusiasm and thoughtful suggestions. And, finally, my gratitude goes to the good folks at Cool Springs Press who thought there was a delicious world for women to explore out there in the backyard.

Table of Contents

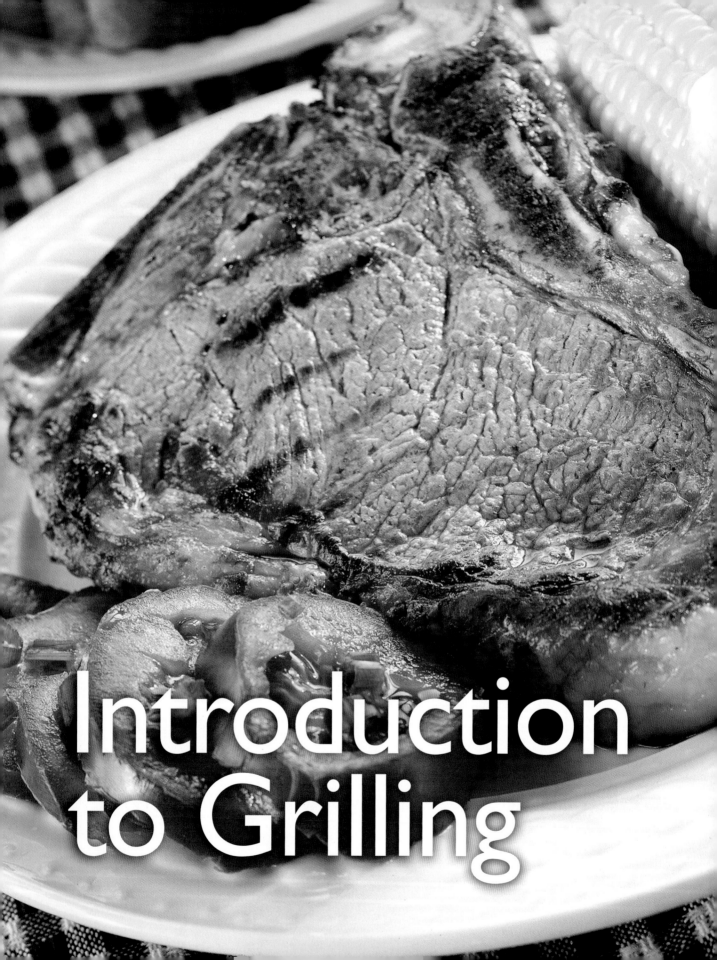

Introduction
to Grilling

What is it about outdoor grilling that sends Moms rushing back into the kitchen to embrace their ovens—where the temperature is always precise—and their stoves—where it's obvious even to the children that the water is, indeed, boiling?

It's fear. Fear of fire. Not that you think you'll catch yourself on fire. No, it's fear that you can't start the fire or control it. It's also fear of failure, a fear that your husband will find you weeping openly as you survey the charred remains of a once beautiful plump chicken.

As a mother, I've discovered that grilling out is actually easier than cooking indoors.

Moms and Grilling

Whether you use a gas or charcoal grill, the only clean-up necessary is accomplished with a wire brush. The grill can produce a spectacular steak or it can be a conveyance for a dandy weenie roast or perfectly charred marshmallows for s'mores. Once you make pizza on a grill, you'll never order carryout again. Getting your children to eat their vegetables becomes a snap when they're cut into chunks and speared onto skewers.

A grill is a multi-purpose tool and a great way to cook an entire meal. You can grill a steak on one part of it while cooking some stuffed portobello mushrooms on another. If you also wrap a few baking potatoes in heavy-duty aluminum foil and stick them on the back of the grill for an hour, you have a complete meal. The grill is also the best tool for quick-as-lightning meals. Marinate some chicken breasts in a store-bought sesame ginger marinade and then grill them in less than 10 minutes.

Use this book creatively. There are lots of variations on the grill, and they'll help make your meals more interesting and varied.

Three Kinds of Recipes

In this book, I have three kinds of recipes: **recipes cooked on the grill, recipes that use leftover grilled food, and recipes that are made on your stove or in your oven and complement grilled foods.**

The recipes that involve just grilling are marked with a **Grilled** banner. The ones that take grilled foods and turn them into something entirely different are marked with the **Leftover** banner. For example, instead of grilling four chicken breasts, grill six. Then use the leftovers for my fabulous chicken salad. Leftover pork tenderloin becomes the star in an easy fried rice recipe.

And then there are recipes that don't involve grilling at all but are hearty accompaniments to grilled food, and they're marked with the **Complement** banner. Pesto red pepper pasta salad just makes grilled chicken wings better. And a steak with my loaded mashed potatoes? Forget about it.

I want you to try all three ways of enjoying a meal with grilled food. I believe grilling shouldn't be a chore—it should just be another valuable tool in your culinary arsenal.

What You'll Learn

Among the pearls of wisdom (maybe not cultured, but pearls nonetheless) that you'll pick up after reading this book are:

My most valuable advice is to start with something easy. Grill some hot dogs. That's a great way to get to know your grill. Then try some chicken wings. Because of the high skin-to-meat ratio, they're very easy to grill without drying out and kids love them. Once you taste the difference between a boiled hot dog and a grilled one, or grilled chicken wings versus fried ones, you'll appreciate the exciting journey in front of you as you experiment with different foods on the grill.

Different types of grills suit different needs, but one thing is always true…**buy the best grill you can afford.** The good ones last for years, far longer than a car (or some husbands). One of my favorites is a portable gas grill that will cook anything from hamburgers to a pork loin, but is small enough to sit on a high table outdoors to keep little fingers away.

Think of your grill as an outdoor oven with groovy wheels. You can precisely gauge the temperature under the dome by using a probe thermometer available at any kitchenware or grill store. If you're using a gas grill, just lay the probe on the grate and adjust the flame to get the temperature you want. On a charcoal grill, make the temperature go up and down by the use of the nifty vents on most grills. I explain this further in Chapter Two, Selecting Your Grill.

The long and sometimes complicated list of ingredients many cookbooks suggest in their recipes for grilling aren't necessary. Juniper berry-studded leg of lamb with port wine reduction and mint foam? I think not. Consider how long those juniper berries will have to sit in the refrigerator before their next time at bat. Instead, I'll give you Master Recipes for fish, fowl, and much more that will then translate into other dishes to enjoy later in the week. Leftovers from a simple marinated grilled flank steak can turn into a spectacular steak salad one day and fajitas the next. Grilled vegetables become a pizza topping or part of a nutritious casserole.

Shortcuts are a good thing. Time-starved moms don't need to add the extra stress of more time in the kitchen preparing to grill. If you don't want to make a marinade from scratch, I'll tell you store-bought alternatives that are as good as homemade. Think that pizza dough will be too complicated? It's not when you buy it at the grocery store, and the nice thing about making your own pizza is that you control the quality of the toppings.

Grills lend themselves to kid-friendly recipes, and children will become more adventurous eaters when they can participate in the process. Present them with chunks of fresh pineapple and ham. Let them build their own meals on wooden skewers and brush with a favorite barbeque sauce. So what if it's a combination you'd never eat. Ten minutes on the grill and they're done (the skewers, not the kids).

Overcome Your Fear

I understand your fear. I was once where you are now. When my son was young, I got my first grill. It was a beautiful gleaming red kettle grill, and I envisioned culinary masterpieces issuing forth from its silvery interior. When he grilled, my father used to wear a jaunty chef's hat with a red checkerboard design around the rim and an apron that said, "Sure, I can cook!" He had no son as the recipient of his expertise, so I learned at the master's knee. I felt I was taking up the family legacy of great grillers with my new kettle.

Not so much. My first outing was an unmitigated disaster. I tried to grill some ribs on my new charcoal grill, but I panicked halfway through when the temperature plummeted. I took them off the grill, ran inside, and put them in the oven. After a few minutes I was filled with remorse, pulled the ribs back out of the oven, added more charcoal to the grill, and slapped those babies back on. My precious son declared they were the best ribs he'd ever eaten. Looking back, they weren't the best, but that day cemented what has become a pleasurable and passionate pastime of cooking over flame.

Once you have tamed your fears, **you will become addicted to this hobby.** You will discover that if one grill is good, two are better. (I have five and I sense more in my future.) You will begin shopping for barbeque gadgets the way you used to shop for shoes (see page 24 for my suggestions on what items you must have). Your refrigerator door will be filled with marinades and your spice drawer with those special barbeque seasonings called rubs (and I have recipes starting on page 30 and suggestions for store-bought spices and seasonings on page 26). Even when the temperature is hovering around freezing, you will have to repress a strong urge to grill a chicken.

I grill out almost every day, but I've taken my passion even further. I'm also a barbecue hobbyist. I'm a Master Certified Judge for the Kansas City Barbecue Society, which sanctions hundreds of barbecue competitions throughout the nation every year. In addition, I'm part of a competition barbecue cooking team, Chicks in Charge. We're an all-girl team (hi, Tatty, Linda, and Mary Ann!). We cook two to three contests a year and have flashes of brilliance. But mostly we just have fun.

Lessons Learned

When you start grilling, not only will you feed your family delicious and nutritious meals, but you'll create valuable family time doing it. We now have a tradition at our house of making pizzas on Friday night. Every member of the family gets to create a special pizza, I put them on the grill, and we enjoy our time together.

I've come a long way from the panic attack of my first grilled ribs. And I've had a lot of fun along the way. I learned that charcoal lighter fluid is a no-no (too dangerous around small children and definitely too smelly). Now I use paraffin starter cubes that work every time. I've learned how to regulate the temperature of the grill using those handy vents that were a mystery to me in the beginning. I've seared steaks at 700 degrees, and they stand up to the ones expensive steakhouses serve, and I've made pork barbeque, cooking it low and slow until it is so tender it melts in your mouth.

I've also discovered that, in some strange way, grilling is relaxing. It's not a bubble bath with champagne, but for me it comes darn close. On a lazy summer evening, I'll put a pork loin on the grill and sit on the deck with a glass of wine, contemplating the good life and the smell of smoke flavored with the musty scent of hard wood charcoal.

Learning to grill is more than a hobby. It will change the way you eat, add more dimension to your menus and, if you play it right, give you some much-needed solitude. ("Children, you must stay inside while mommy's lighting the grill!")

Enjoy the guilty pleasure of doing something you'd never allow your children to do—learning to play with fire and eating the delicious results!

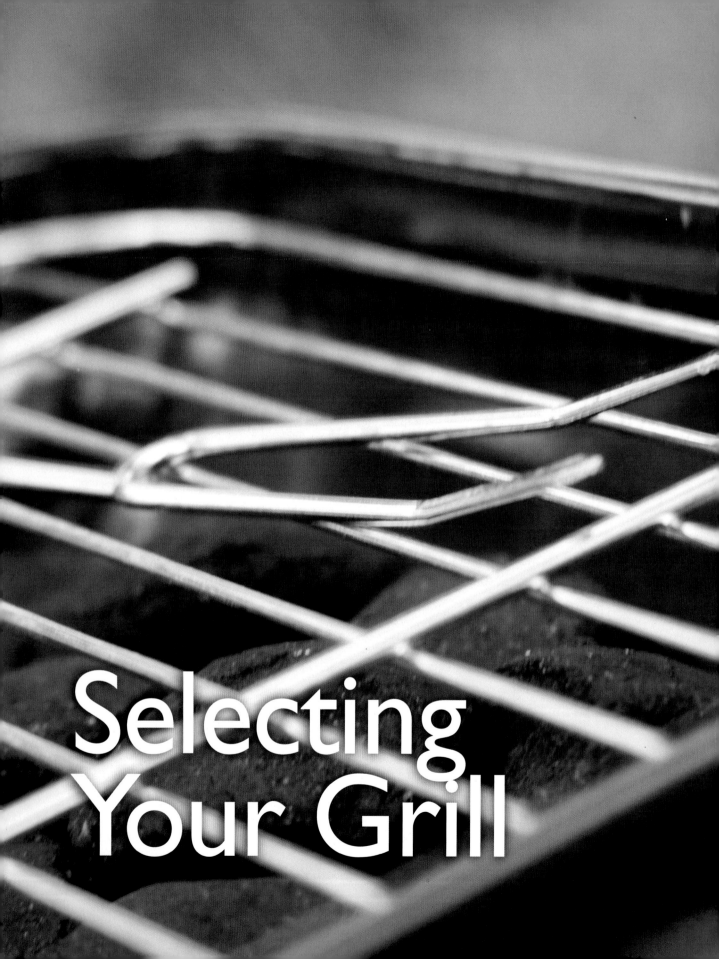

Selecting Your Grill

Here's what I want you to remember above all else, girls. Grilling is not a science. There are a lot of variables that will influence your final product—how hot the fire is, how thick the meat is, whether you add a glaze or not. The big thing here is just to relax.

Just like any new piece of equipment, you'll have to get used to your grill. If it's gas, go ahead, light it, and play with the knobs. Breathe in, breathe out. If your new grill is charcoal, go ahead and start a fire even if you don't plan on cooking. Close the lid and play with the vents. Breathe in, breathe out. It's going to be fun!

Charcoal Versus Gas

There are only two ways to go when you are grilling—charcoal or gas. Each has its virtues and its drawbacks.

Gas grilling is the easiest. You just turn on the propane, light the burners, and away you go. Because most mothers are short on time, gas may be the easiest way to start your grilling career; it takes the same amount of time to turn on the grill as it does the stove, and it's just as easy to maintain a precise temperature.

The drawback to gas is that the rich smoky flavor that comes from hardwood charcoal is absent. (There are ways to introduce that flavor through wood chips or pellets, and we'll get to that in a minute.)

The other method of grilling is with charcoal. It's slightly more time consuming because you have to wait for the coals to ash over after the fire is lit. And instead of controlling the temperature with a knob, as you do on a gas grill, you have to control it using the vents on the grill. It takes a little more practice, but mastering a fire of live coals can be immensely rewarding.

Here are the basic, no-fail ways to start for both methods.

Starting Your Gas Grill

Every gas grill needs a tank of propane, which is sold at most home improvement stores. **When you set up your grill, read the instructions.** You will hook up the propane with a hose (not your garden hose!) that comes with the grill.

Hot Tips

If your gas grill has a cabinet enclosing the propane tank, leave one of the doors open the first few times you grill. The open door will remind you to turn the propane off after you're done.

14

Turn on the grill. This is a two-step process. First you turn the nozzle of the propane tank to "open." It will say that right on the knob. *Make sure the grill lid is open.* Once you turn on the propane, there are two ways to light the grill. If you have a gas grill with an automatic starter, just press it in as you turn the knob. If you don't have an automatic starter, turn on the grill as you hold a long-necked lighter to the gas burner. It will ignite. You can then adjust the temperature of the grill and close the lid to warm it up for a few minutes. When you are finished, just reverse the process. Turn the grill off and then turn the propane tank off. *Remember to turn the propane off!* (Here's how I remember: If you turn the knob all the way to "on," then when your grilling is done, it's easy to remember to turn the knob all the way to "off." Also, I leave one of the grill doors where the propane sits open just to jog my memory.)

Some gas grills have a smoking chamber where you can add wood. If you want to introduce a wood flavor to your food, buy some wood *chips* or *pellets* from a manufacturer such as BBQr's Delight™. For the *chips,* take a handful and soak them in water for 30 minutes. That will allow the chips to smolder and create more smoke in your grill. Put them in the smoking chamber and heat the grill. On the other hand, *do not* soak the *pellets* because they will disintegrate! Instead, place about 1/3 cup in a square of tin foil. Enclose as a packet, and poke a small hole in the packet with a toothpick. You won't believe how much smoke will come out of that little hole. Most wood flavors will be fine for whatever you grill. Oak and hickory are always good, while fruit woods and pecan impart a milder flavor. Do not use mesquite on anything but beef because it will make the food bitter.

Starting Your Charcoal Grill

The first thing is the charcoal. You want one of two kinds only. **Either buy pure lump charcoal, which is actually wood that has been burned until it forms charcoal lumps, or buy a pure briquette such as Kingsford® Charcoal.** You do not want charcoal that has been soaked in lighter fluid. (It will leave a terrible taste in your food and it's dangerous to have around children.)

Lighting a charcoal grill is almost as easy as lighting a gas grill. Load the grill with charcoal. Use more than you think you should. **One of the biggest complaints by new charcoal grillers is that the fire isn't hot enough, and that's usually because there wasn't enough charcoal in the grill.** Nestle two or three fire starters (made of paraffin or wood and available at grilling and outdoor stores) between the charcoal and light with your long-necked lighter. *Do not close the lid!* Fire likes air. Keep the lid open until the charcoal acquires a gray ashy coating.

You can also use a chimney to start your coals, but I think they're more trouble than they're worth now that the fire starter cubes are available.

Controlling the temperature is harder on a charcoal grill. It takes practice, and I'd recommend the first time you light your charcoal grill that you spend about 30 minutes just playing with the temperature of the fire. Just remember: Fire likes air. The more air you give fire, the hotter it will get. And also remember that it's easier to make a fire hotter than it is to lower the temperature once the charcoal is raging. So put a probe thermometer (just the shiny, pointy part; the part that actually measures the temperature—not the whole thing) on the top of the grill, close the lid, and play with the vents. Close the vents almost all the way, and note the temperature after a few minutes. Now open them halfway, and note the temperature after a few minutes. Once you've finished cooking, close the lid and close all the vents. No air—no fire.

What You Need in a Grill

With either gas or charcoal there are certain things you should look for when you buy your grill.

I have five grills—three charcoal and two gas. I don't use them all the time, but somehow I feel comforted having them around. My dream grill would be that big mamma-jamma monster with warming drawers and a prep area. That will be coming right after my husband acquires the antique Chris Craft boat he wants to restore.

Gas Grills

Just as with everything else in life, you get what you pay for. Considering that you'll be using this grill just like you use your stove, you want to get as much grill as you can for the money.

Burners. You need to get a grill with at least two burners if you are going to do indirect cooking, which is like using the grill as an oven.

Material. Look for a grill that is heavy for its size. You want as much insulation in the metal as you can get. Stainless steel is the material of choice for a lot of grills, but make sure the entire grill is made of stainless. Some grills with a stainless body have internal legs made from another material that could rust.

Grates. Try to find a grill that has porcelain-coated, cast-iron grates. Cast iron is one of the best heat conductors you can get, and the porcelain coating makes it easier to clean because it doesn't let food stick as much.

BTUs. This is where the eyes of most women glaze over, including me. But stick with me a minute. What's a BTU? It's a British Thermal Unit. Your grill will have a BTU rating, which is basically how hot the grill will get when all the burners are turned on for an hour. As BTUs go, a higher rating may not be better. It also depends on how the grill in constructed and whether it retains heat well. When I buy a grill, I go to Consumer Reports to see what it recommends. They do nothing but test stuff and then tell consumers which ones got the best ratings. Also, go to a reputable grill dealer and get his or her opinion about the best grill for you.

Side burners. Many grills have side burners for heating sauces or side dishes. Personally, I don't mind an extra burner because the lid that closes over it just adds extra shelf space to the grill. But I have never yet used the actual burner. My kitchen is close to the deck where I grill, and it's easier to use the stove for heating things than it is to cart the pot out to the grill.

Shelf space below the grill. Your propane tank will go underneath the grill in most models. But look and see how much extra space there is for grilling tools and supplies.

A built-in thermometer. Even though you're going to be using a probe thermometer to take the internal temperature of meat, it's also nice to see what the internal temperature of the grill is, just as it's nice to know how hot your oven is. Remember, however, that the

Hot Tips

Think of your grill as a combination of oven and stove. When you want to grill over indirect heat, it's as though you're using an oven. When you want to cook the food directly over the flame, it's just like using your stove.

thermometer will register how hot it is at the top of the grill (heat rises and the end of the thermometer is at the top of the grill). The grate-level temperature will be slightly different. By the way, don't get too hung up on grate- or dome-level temperatures. We're cooking food, here. We're not conducting science experiments.

Charcoal Grills

Some of what you need in a charcoal grill is the same as in a gas grill.

Heavy-duty construction. This is the major thing you want to look for in a charcoal grill. The thinner the sides and top of the grill, the less heat it will hold. If you lift the lid of a grill and think, "Gee, that sure is light," then pass it by and find one where the lid has some heft.

Cooking capacity. You want to be able to grill both directly (think stove top) and indirectly (think oven). So you need enough room to build not only an even bed of coals for direct cooking, but also a banked set of coals for indirect cooking.

Vents. Be sure to look for the number of vents. If the grill has no vents, walk on by. Vents are the means by which you control the heat. Remember, if the vents are open, it translates to high heat, and if the vents are partially closed, it translates to lower heat. Vents closed (and lid down) means you're putting the fire out—and that's how you do it when you're finished cooking.

Hinged grate. Sometimes when you're cooking you'll need to add additional charcoal, and a hinged grate allows you to do that.

By far the best-selling charcoal grill is the Weber® kettle. It looks like a bowl on legs, and the construction allows the heat to be concentrated and produce an intense fire when needed and a low and slow fire when required. It is built like a fortress, and it's not uncommon for Weber kettles to last the lifetime of the griller and beyond. Instead of the family jewels, you can bequeath a Weber kettle to your offspring.

Don't feel you have to spend big bucks on a grill. You can buy a hibachi, which is a lot of grill for a little money. The only drawback is that it doesn't have a large grilling surface. But for a family of three it will do, and it's a great grill to learn on.

The top-of-the-line charcoal grills for my money are ceramic cookers, particularly the Big Green Egg®. After a lifetime of grilling, my husband gave me a large Big Green Egg for Christmas one year and it was better than a diamond tennis bracelet (well, almost).

Ceramic cookers can grill low or slow for barbeque, or incredibly high for searing steaks and making pizza that rivals any pizza house you can imagine. Because it holds heat incredibly well, it uses very little charcoal. And temperature control is a snap.

The drawbacks to ceramic cookers are that they're expensive and they're heavy. Once you get your ceramic cooker on the patio or deck, it will stay there until you sell the house (and maybe afterward).

The other thing about charcoal grills that you must remember to do is to remove the ash that results from burning coals. You should clean out the ash pan under the grill after every use to ensure that the grill is operating at maximum efficiency. But do this after the grill has cooled because sometimes small bits of live coals can make their way into the ash pan.

You also need to remember to stir the cold leftover charcoal after every couple of uses to get the excess ash out of the grill. Charcoal grills have a pan at the bottom to hold excess ash. You'll also have to periodically dump the excess ash out of the pan.

After you have checked off all the "should haves" on your grill selection, let your female intuition step in. If you love that big stainless steel grill with the side shelves and it's not going to bust the budget, go ahead and splurge. Your grill is not just a purchase; it's an investment that should last you many happy years.

Starting an Indirect Fire

Whether you're using a gas grill or a charcoal one, at some point you will need to build an indirect fire. Remember, a direct fire is like using your stove—the heat is applied directly to the cooking vessel or food. **An indirect fire is like your oven.** The heat doesn't directly touch the food.

Starting an indirect fire in your gas grill is easy. Just turn on half the burners, and use the grates on the other half of the grill for gentler cooking. You would do this if you're grilling garlic bread, for instance. You want to just heat the bread through, not char the bottom of it.

In a charcoal grill, it's almost as simple. Bank your charcoal against one side of the grill, leaving just a few coals on the other side. Light the pile with fire starter cubes. Whatever you want to cook indirectly, put it over the side with the least coals.

Cleaning Your Grill

Some men maintain that you never have to clean a grill. They may scrape off the crusty bits that adhere to the grate once every five years, but they never actually clean a grill.

They're wrong. Especially with gas grills, you do have to apply a bit of routine maintenance every once in awhile. A woman's fine-honed ability to discern what constitutes "dirty" will help you know when it's time. For me, it's when I look through the grill grate and say "Icky" as I look at what's accumulated on the gas vent tops.

Bear in mind that you'll never get a grill completely clean. It's not like an oven. Some of those crispy bits will never, ever come off.

Here's my routine for grill cleaning. First, get a pair of those handy latex gloves. It's a dirty job, but not as bad if your hands are protected.

Gas grills. First, take the grates and the gas vent tops off the grill. With a grill scraper, scrape the crusty bits in the bottom of the grill into the hole over the grease trap.

Empty the grease trap. It's that tray in the back of the grill that collects grease from cooking. When it's cool, empty what you can into a plastic bag and set the dirty trap aside.

Spread some newspaper on your deck or patio. Put the grates and the gas vent tops on the newspaper and scrape off whatever gunk will come off easily by hand. Spray the grates and vent tops with a heavy-duty cleaner. I use Goo Gone® BBQ Grill Cleaner, but anything that cuts grease will do.

Let the grease remover work for 10 to 15 minutes before you wipe it off with paper towels. Then, using a garden hose with a high-powered nozzle, spray the vent tops and grates to remove the rest of the cleaner. Be sure you dry the vent tops and grates before returning them to the grill.

Charcoal grills. They are easier to clean. The only thing you really need to clean is the cooking grate, using the same method as with a gas grill. And, once again, empty the ash pan every once in awhile.

You also need to check the inside of the lid every so often. Because you're using charcoal, a layer of soot can build up inside the lid and you'll need to wipe that clean.

If you live in a warm, humid climate (like almost everywhere during the summer) and you keep your grill covered, it's possible to get a little bit of mold build-up on the inside of the grill. Just wipe it with a damp paper towel and then dry the area.

Hot Tips

**When you turn on the grill, close
the lid and wait 20 to 30 minutes to make sure
the grill is uniformly hot.**

**Keep your grill-cleaning tool right next to the grill.
When you've finished cooking, clean the grate right away. It's easier
to get any residue off the grate while the grill is still hot.**

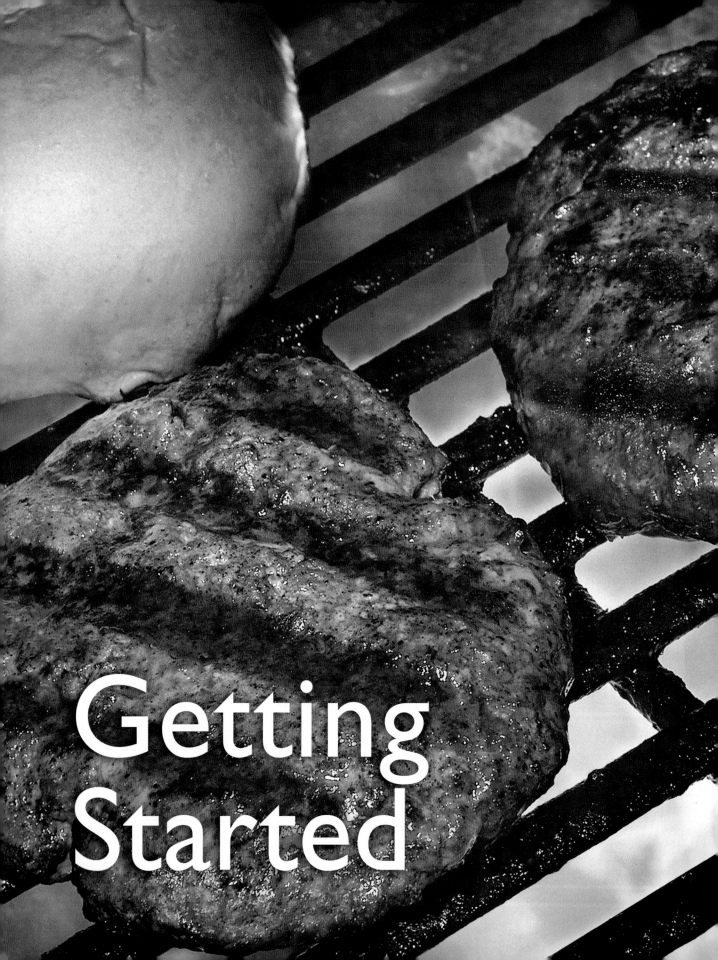

Getting
Started

Just as you have a favorite set of pans for the stove, there are certain grilling items you'll use over and over again. In my house, I have a separate drawer for my grilling tools so they're easy to find at a moment's notice.

I am from the "less is more" school when it comes to collecting cooking implements in general. I shy away from gadgets that only do one job (does anyone really need a hot dog cooker?). I look for tools that will do multiple jobs. If I find something, like tongs, that I use grilling *and* when I cook inside, I really like it.

Grilling Gadgets

When my son was in grade school, he would eye every item in the checkout line at the grocery store and beg for a donation to the Noah Chapin Mayhew Sugar Rush Fund. After awhile, I started telling him there was a difference between "needs" and "wants."

Let me break up the proliferation of grilling gadgets into "needs" and "wants" so you can tell when you've crossed the line from an enthusiast to an addict.

Here's what you need.

A good set of tongs. Tongs are those long-armed metal things with a spring at the end. You can find them at grilling shops, but don't buy those. They tend to be hard to handle and don't grasp food securely. Go to your local general merchandise store and buy a pair for about $5. You will use your tongs to add, remove, and turn food on the grill. You will grow to love your tongs so much you will use them in all your cooking. Note: They also make outstanding devices to chase your children with when they're naughty.

A probe thermometer. You can find these at grilling stores also, but they tend to be horribly expensive. Go to a general merchandise store and pick one up for less than $20. That

Hot Tips

Join fellow grillers online for help and advice. Two good grilling bulletin boards are www.grillforum.com and www.eggheadforum.com. (The latter is primarily for those who own a Big Green Egg, but there's lots of great general advice as well.)

Grilling can be messy. Invest in a box of good disposable latex gloves you can wear for everything from lifting greasy grates to picking up marinated foods going on the grill. After, you can just toss them. (I get mine from www.drugstore.com.)

may still sound like a lot of cash, but your probe thermometer will become your new best friend. Read the instruction book (I know, what a drag) so you know how to operate it. The probe is inserted into meat on the grill so you can tell if it's done, in the case of chicken, or done to your liking, in the case of beef. You can also use it to test the temperature at grate level on the grill.

A long-necked lighter. You can find these at any supermarket in the charcoal aisle. Get more than one. You'll find a million uses for them.

Insulated gloves. These you may have to go to a barbecue store to find. They are not fashion items, but they will protect your hands if, for instance, you realize after you've started your fire that you forgot to add wood chips and have to lift the grate up (this is from experience, trust me). They are as good as potholders or better when you need to remove dishes from the grill.

Fire starters. If you are cooking on a charcoal grill, these are essential. They come as either paraffin-type cubes or what looks to me like wooden particleboard. Both work. You just nestle them in the charcoal and light them. They do the job 100 percent of the time. Do not use charcoal lighter fluid. Ever. You can let the coals burn until pigs fly, but you'll never get that gassy smell and taste out of your food. And, more importantly, charcoal lighter fluid is high on the list of dangerous items to have around the house, right behind machetes and hand grenades.

A can of cooking spray. Grill grates are a lot easier to clean up if you spray them with oil first. Enough said.

A wire brush. Go for the sturdiest one you can find. Once you're done grilling, give the grate a vigorous scrub with the brush while the grill is still hot. It's much easier to get any bits of food that have crusted onto the grate off that way.

Heavy-duty foil. Do not buy anything else. You will find a million additional uses for heavy-duty foil, but you must have it for various grilling techniques.

A grill cover. Grills can get nasty looking quickly without a good grill cover. Be religious about covering the grill as soon as it cools down. A grill cover will extend the life of what was probably a pretty significant purchase.

A grilling basket. There are several types of grilling baskets. An open basket where you can turn the food is the best. You use them for items that would otherwise slip through the grill grates such as sliced vegetables. Some grilling baskets come with a long handle and a square grill box with an expandable, lockable lid. The problem with this style is that the handle is flush with only one side of the basket so it's impossible to turn it over and still close the lid on the grill. I found this out through sorry experimentation with one. Do not try to be thrifty here. If you buy a grill basket for $5, it will behave like the cheap sorry product it is. Invest in a good one and it will last a lifetime.

Here are some items that are nice to have but not essential.

A kabob basket. The good news is that kabob baskets keep all the ingredients locked in long rectangular boxes so that nothing can slide around. The bad news is they have the same problem as the lockable lid grilling baskets. You can't turn them over and close the grill. The other problem is that even though they are coated with a "non-stick" coating, they are a bear to clean. And no mom needs any more work cleaning up. But there are times when you'll be glad you have a kabob basket.

Metal skewers. If you're making kabobs, metal skewers are better than bamboo ones. They last a lifetime, and there's no chance they'll burn up on the grill. I have soaked bamboo skewers in water until they're about to explode and sometimes they still catch fire.

A rotisserie attachment for your grill. I have one and it's fun to play with. The rotisserie makes a terrific whole chicken or wonderful Cornish game hens. But it's not the kind of thing you'll use every day.

Spices and Rubs

Spices and rubs give flavor to meat. Most cooks don't use enough seasoning on their food. When you think you have enough, add a little more.

I'm not a big fan of acquiring huge stocks of spices and rubs you won't use more than a few times. That's why I don't recommend too many specific varieties in this book. In many cases, salt and pepper will suffice, and in Chapter Four, I offer for recipes for seasonings that are quick and easy to make.

But I do have a few brands I go back to again and again. Most of them are not widely available. I've found them through one of my passionate hobbies, which is competition barbecuing (it's the opposite of grilling, which is hot and fast cooking—barbecuing is low and slow cooking). I've transferred their use to the grill with great results.

Hot Tips

Some propane tanks come with a built-in reserve. When you're about to run out of propane, the gas flow stops. You flip a switch, relight your grill, and it comes back on with about an hour of fuel left. If you can't find those tanks, be sure to have an extra propane tank on hand. Nothing is worse than being halfway through cooking a steak and running out of gas.

If your kids are old enough to use the stove, they're old enough to use the grill. Teaching them how to cook—both indoors and out—will pay big dividends when they're out on their own.

Always sharpen your kitchen knives every time you use them. A dull knife is far more dangerous than a sharp one.

I have no financial stake in the list below (although I wish I did!). These are just my favorites and where you can get them at printing time.

Cavender's All Purpose Greek Seasoning®. Great on anything, but especially on beef. Widely available in grocery stores.

McCormick's® Grill Mates® Montreal Steak Seasoning. I use it for beef, chicken, and pork. I have also used it with seafood such as shrimp. It's widely available in grocery stores.

Steven Raichlen's Java Barbecue Rub. This is an outstanding rub for pork tenderloin. You wouldn't think coffee would be good in a spice rub, but it really brings out the flavor of the meat. Available on **Amazon.com** or by searching the Web under its name.

Papa Tony's New Orleans Style Shrimp Mix. It's great with shrimp, but also good with chicken. Available at **www.papatonys.net**.

Dizzy Dust. This all-purpose rub is made by Chris Capell, part of the award-winning Dizzy Pig BBQ tem. Find it at **www.dizzypigbbq.com**.

Bobbie's Barbecue Seasoning and Rub. A good all-purpose seasoning that adds a little sweetness to meat, poultry and seafood. Available at **www.pigpals.net**.

Bad Byron's Butt Rub® Barbecue Seasoning. An assertive seasoning for beef and pork especially. Available at **www.buttrub.com**. If you love peanuts, try Butt Rub's addictive barbecue seasoning roasted peanuts.

Obie-Cue's Sweet Rub BBQ Spice. Terrific on pork and chicken. Available at **www.hawgeyesbbq.com** or **www.obiecue.com**.

Pantry Favorites

I am not a big fan of specialty ingredients. I hardly ever use recipes that call for an ingredient I will use only once-in-a-blue-moon. Most chefs will tell you that the best food is food simply prepared. I'm no chef, but I subscribe to that theory.

There are certain items I always have in my pantry and refrigerator. They can do double or triple duty. At the end of a long day, the last thing I want to do is start some complicated recipe with multiple steps and a long ingredient list with items I don't have.

Here's what I keep on hand all the time and some of their uses.

Extra-virgin olive oil. Get the good stuff. You can tell the difference. I use it for marinades, salad dressings, to sauté meats and vegetables, and as a dip seasoned with dried herb mixes for crusty bread.

Butter. Yes, real butter. Just like extra-virgin olive oil, it's the good stuff. I'm not advocating that you use a stick of it every time you cook, but nothing else can come close to the flavor of real butter. I buy it in four carton packages at the local warehouse store and freeze it. I use it half-and-half with olive oil to sauté almost anything. I also use a judicious amount in my scrambled eggs for breakfast—you have all day to work it off.

Vinegar. Be it cider, red wine, balsamic, or champagne, I love vinegar. I use it to whip up a quick vinaigrette for salads. Balsamic is good drizzled over a salad of tomatoes and fresh mozzarella cheese.

Garlic. I love it in almost any marinade, minced and sautéed for vegetables, and added to salad dressings. If you're using it in a sauté, remember to only cook it for about 30 seconds because if it burns it becomes bitter. I always add it at the end of the sautéing time even if the recipe disagrees.

Onions. Red or white, Spanish or sweet—onions make everything taste better.

Lemons. Lemons give everything zip. I add lemon juice to dips and spreads. I also squeeze some into a sauté pan with melted butter before adding vegetables.

Dried seasoned breadcrumbs. They come in a round container and are usually found on the baking aisle. Use them for stuffed mushrooms, in meatloaf, and browned with butter and lemon over vegetables.

Worcestershire and soy sauce. Both add a saltiness and depth of flavor to many marinades, sauces, dips, and spreads.

Sea or kosher salt and whole peppercorns in grinders. You can get small versions of these in the spice aisle at the grocery store or giant-sized ones at super discount stores such as Costco or Sam's.

Simple bottled marinades such as Dale's or Moore's Original. They're handy for quickly marinating a steak without making a homemade marinade.

Seasonings and Sauces

The most common mistake most new cooks make is not seasoning food enough. Case in point—the humble hamburger. Even if you're going to load on the condiments when the burger is cooked, the raw meat itself needs to be seasoned. The general rule of thumb is one teaspoon of salt for every pound of hamburger.

Almost any kind of grilled food needs a little boost from a spice rub, marinade, or dipping sauce. These are some ideas for sauces you can make, but don't be afraid to create your own special seasonings or use commercially made ones from the grocery store.

Mayhew's Special Seasoning

This is an all-purpose blend you can use for any meat, poultry, fish, or vegetable. It has a little more kick than salt and pepper, but if you don't have time to mix up a batch, just remember that salt and pepper are still God's gifts to seasoning anything. You can buy black pepper already coarsely ground.

> 1/4 **cup salt**
> 1 **teaspoon coarsely ground black pepper**
> 1 **teaspoon garlic powder**
> 1 **teaspoon onion powder**
> 1/2 **teaspoon paprika**

❖ Combine the salt, pepper, garlic powder, onion powder and paprika in a small bowl and mix well.

❖ Note: There's a difference between garlic powder and garlic salt. Read the label!

❖ Yields about 1/2 cup.

Hot Tips

Spices hate light. To extend the life of your
spices, either store them in a dark cabinet or, better
yet, store them in the freezer.

Barbecue Dipping Sauce

Barbecue sauce is an individual thing—play with this basic recipe and add your own touches. This dipping sauce goes well with Cocktail Weenie Kabobs (see page 67).

   1 tablespoon olive oil
   ½ cup chopped yellow onion
   1 cup ketchup
   ¼ cup firmly packed brown sugar
   2 tablespoons prepared yellow mustard
   1 tablespoon Worcestershire sauce
   ½ teaspoon salt

❖ Heat the olive oil in a medium saucepan over medium heat on the stove. Sauté the onion in the hot oil for 5 minutes or until translucent. Add the ketchup, brown sugar, mustard, Worcestershire sauce and salt; mix well. Cook over low heat for about 10 minutes or until very warm, stirring occasionally.

❖ Yields about 1½ cups.

Asian Dipping Sauce

This simple sauce goes great with the Moo-Shu Pork Won Tons (see page 68) or any Asian dumpling. If you're cooking for a crowd, just double or triple the recipe. The ingredients can be found in the international food aisle of your grocery store.

1 1/2 tablespoons hoisin sauce
3 tablespoons soy sauce
10 drops dark sesame oil

❖ Combine the hoisin sauce, soy sauce and sesame oil in a small bowl; whisk until smooth. Serve at room temperature.

❖ Yields about 1/3 cup.

Mustard Dill Sauce

This sauce is great with salmon or chicken.

1/2 cup sour cream
1 tablespoon Dijon mustard
1 tablespoon snipped dill
1/8 teaspoon salt

❖ Place the sour cream, Dijon mustard, dill and salt in a small bowl and mix well. Chill, covered, for at least 1 hour before serving.

❖ Yields about 1/2 cup.

Butter Dipping Sauce for Shrimp

This simple sauce works well for crab or lobster as well as shrimp. If you can't find chipotle pepper sauce, any hot sauce can be used to give the butter a slightly spicy bite.

> 1/2 cup (1 stick) butter
> 1 large or 2 small garlic cloves, minced
> 1 teaspoon chipotle pepper sauce

❖ Melt the butter in a small sauté pan on the stove. Stir in the garlic and pepper sauce. Cook the butter mixture over low heat for about 10 minutes or until the garlic has softened.

❖ Yields 1/2 cup.

Cajun Tartar Sauce

If your kids don't like capers, you can use pickle relish in this recipe. This sauce works well with grilled catfish (see page 106).

> 1/2 cup mayonnaise
> 1 tablespoon grainy mustard
> 1/2 teaspoon Worcestershire sauce
> 1/2 teaspoon Cajun seasoning
> 1 teaspoon fresh lemon juice
> 2 teaspoons capers
> 1/8 teaspoon salt

❖ Combine the mayonnaise, mustard, Worcestershire sauce, Cajun seasoning, lemon juice, capers and salt in a small bowl and blend well. Chill for at least 1 hour before serving.

❖ Yields about 1/2 cup.

Seafood Dipping Sauce

The horseradish gives this sauce a little zip—if your children don't like spicy foods, you can leave out the horseradish.

1 cup sour cream
¼ cup ketchup
1 teaspoon creamy horseradish
1 teaspoon fresh lemon juice
1 teaspoon Worcestershire sauce
½ teaspoon salt
¼ teaspoon celery seed

❖ Combine the sour cream, ketchup, horseradish, lemon juice, Worcestershire sauce, salt and celery seed in a medium bowl; mix well. Chill, covered, until serving time. Serve with grilled or boiled shrimp.

❖ Yields about 1 cup.

Olive Oil Dipping Sauce

Use this sauce with grilled Pizza Sticks (see page 127) or any good crusty bread.

> 1/2 **cup extra-virgin olive oil**
> 2 **tablespoons grated Parmesan cheese**
> 1 **tablespoon dried oregano**
> 1 **teaspoon hot red pepper flakes**
> 1/2 **teaspoon freshly ground black pepper**

❖ Combine the olive oil, Parmesan cheese, oregano, red pepper flakes and black pepper in a small bowl; mix well. This sauce may stand, covered, at room temperature for several days.

❖ Yields about 1/2 cup.

Red Wine Marinade

This is a good marinade for any beef or lamb dish.

> 1/2 **cup dry red wine**
> 1/4 **cup extra-virgin olive oil**
> 2 **tablespoons Worcestershire sauce**
> 2 **tablespoons fresh lemon juice**
> 2 **garlic cloves, thinly sliced**

❖ Combine the wine, olive oil, Worcestershire sauce, lemon juice and garlic in a large glass dish and whisk well. Add the meat. Marinate, covered, in the refrigerator for 4 to 10 hours. Drain the meat and remove the garlic slices before grilling.

❖ Yields about 1 cup.

Herb Butter

You can use this butter in a lot of ways. It's decadent on top of a sizzling steak. It makes a great sauce for pasta. Keep it in the refrigerator or freezer, and use it as the occasion inspires you.

**¹⁄₂ cup (1 stick) butter, at room temperature
1 tablespoon each minced fresh parsley,
minced fresh chives and fresh thyme leaves**

❖ Place the butter in a small bowl. Blend in the parsley, chives and thyme. Wrap the butter mixture in plastic wrap and shape into a log. Chill, tightly wrapped, in the refrigerator.

❖ Yields ¹⁄₂ cup.

Basic Vinaigrette

I almost never buy salad dressings. I prefer salad just lightly coated with vinaigrette so the taste of the lettuce shines through. I love the white balsamic flavor, but you can use any kind of vinegar. You can also substitute shallots for the garlic if your kids prefer a milder taste.

**1 tablespoon white balsamic vinegar
2 teaspoons Dijon mustard
1 small garlic clove, minced
¹⁄₂ teaspoon salt
¹⁄₄ teaspoon pepper
4 tablespoons extra-virgin olive oil**

❖ Combine the vinegar, Dijon mustard, garlic, salt and pepper in a small glass bowl and whisk to blend. Whisk in the olive oil slowly until the mixture is emulsified.

❖ Yields ¹⁄₂ cup.

Brine Complement

Brine offers a simple way to add loads of moisture to lean meats such as chicken or turkey. I also use it for lean pork chops. Just immerse your meat in the brine and refrigerate for up to 4 hours.

2 quarts water
¼ cup kosher salt
¼ cup firmly packed dark brown sugar
I bay leaf
2 garlic cloves, peeled

❖ Heat the water in a 2-quart kettle over medium heat on the stove, or microwave two 4-cup measuring cups of water on High for 3 minutes each. Add the kosher salt and stir to dissolve. Add the brown sugar, bay leaf and garlic; stir to dissolve the brown sugar. Let stand until completely cool.

❖ Yields enough brine for I turkey breast or 4 chicken breasts.

Hot Tips

**If you're making brine, after combining
all the ingredients thoroughly, stick it in the freezer
to help it cool quicker.**

Roasted Red Pepper Sauce

This is a great sauce with grilled chicken or fish. You could roast your own red peppers on the grill, but sometimes easier is better. A jar of roasted red peppers cuts out a lot of time and effort.

1 (12-ounce) jar roasted red peppers, drained
1/2 cup sour cream
1/2 cup mayonnaise
1 teaspoon Worcestershire sauce

❖ Place the peppers in a food processor container and process until coarsely chopped; drain if there is any excess juice. Combine the chopped peppers, sour cream, mayonnaise and Worcestershire sauce in a small bowl and mix well. Chill, covered, for 30 minutes or longer.

❖ Yields about 1 cup.

Hot Tips

Spices and rubs give flavor to meat. Most cooks
don't use enough seasoning on their food. When you
think you have enough, add a little more.

Easy Tomato Sauce

Every cook should have a basic tomato sauce recipe. It's not only good for pasta, but also with grilled meats. Use your imagination, and make a casserole of leftover grilled chicken, penne pasta, tomato sauce, and mozzarella cheese.

¼ **cup extra-virgin olive oil**
½ **cup chopped onion**
1 **garlic clove, minced**
¼ **cup shredded carrots**
Salt and pepper to taste
1 **(32-ounce) can crushed tomatoes**
2 **bay leaves**
1 **tablespoon dried oregano**

❖ Heat the olive oil in a 2-quart kettle over medium-high heat on the stove. Sauté the onion in the hot oil until translucent. Add the garlic and carrots and sauté for about 30 seconds longer. Season with salt and pepper. Stir in the crushed tomatoes, bay leaves and oregano. Simmer, uncovered, for 30 minutes to 1 hour.

❖ Yields about 4 cups.

Master
Recipes

The best way to enjoy the great taste of grilled food is not to spend a lot of time worrying over the grill.

The natural tendency of most women when they start to grill is to hover. Hover over the charcoal to see if it's lit. Hover over the grill when the food is on. Flip up the lid. Stare at the meat. Is it ready to turn? You make yourself crazy.

That's why we're starting our trip down incendiary lane with some master recipes.

Easy Recipes as You Learn

Master recipes aren't meant to be the most complicated thing you'll ever grill. In fact, it's quite the opposite. These recipes should be the simplest things you grill. (In the Meat and Poultry chapter, I offer variations on these simple master recipes.)

I want you to get comfortable with the grill, and to do that, I don't want you sweating the big stuff. The first time, try these recipes as I've written them. They are recipes I make for my family all the time, so I know they work.

Please note that if a recipe calls for a 1-inch steak, it's because I measured the steak I was cooking at the time just for this book and that's how thick it was. It doesn't mean you have to spend hours in the grocery store measuring your meat. If your steak is a little thinner, cook it a little less.

Hot Tips

Meats with a high fat content (such as lamb chops and some steaks) will cause flare-ups in the grill when the melting fat hits the coals or heating element. If the flames get too scary, use your tongs to move the meat to a cooler part of the grill.

When you're grilling meats with bones in warm weather, wrap the leftover bones in heavy-duty aluminum foil and put them in the freezer until garbage day. That way your garbage cans won't stink.

Never place cooked meat on the platter that held it when it was uncooked.

I used to completely obsess about whether chicken, in particular, was done. That's why I love those probe thermometers—they take all the guesswork out. For some of these recipes, you'll also need heavy-duty gloves, tongs, and a grill basket. (Check out page 24 for my advice on which grilling tools are necessary and which ones are optional.)

Temperatures

One of the scariest parts of grilling for beginners is telling how hot the grill is. There's an easy way to do this called the "hand" method, which simply means how long can you hold your hand 6 inches from the heat before you say "ouch!"

- **High heat:** 500 degrees and you'll be able to leave your hand over the grate for 3 seconds.
- **Medium-high heat:** 400 degrees or about 5 seconds.
- **Medium heat:** 350 degrees or about 7 seconds.
- **Medium-low:** 325 degrees or 10 seconds.
- **Low heat:** 300 degrees or 12 seconds.

Do not trust the built-in thermometers that come installed on some grills. Some of them are highly accurate; others are not. If you absolutely want to know the temperature at grate level, put the metal end of a probe thermometer on the grate and close the lid. Wait about 5 minutes and take a reading.

Also remember to use the "palm" method while checking steaks and pork for doneness. Tense up the fleshy part of your hand under the thumb. It sort of feels like a squishy tennis ball. That's medium-rare. A little firmer is medium; a little softer is rare. Or use your probe thermometer to check the internal temperature of the meat. (Be sure you put the tip of the thermometer in the thickest part of the meat without touching a bone.)

Once you've gotten comfortable with these master recipes, vary them to add your own special touches. Try different glazes, marinades, and rubs. Create your own special magic at the grill!

T-Bone Steaks ⟩ Grilled

With any kind of steak, simple preparations are best. Why mess up a good piece of meat by overthinking the recipe? T-bones are my favorite because you get a wonderful piece of top loin and a bit of tenderloin as an added bonus. I have designed this recipe for two. T-bones are expensive, and the kids wouldn't appreciate the budgetary sacrifice.

2 (1-inch-thick) T-bone steaks
Mayhew's Special Seasoning (see page 32)
Nonstick cooking spray

❖ Let the steaks stand at room temperature for about 30 minutes. Season them liberally with Special Seasoning.

❖ Heat the grill to at least 500 degrees. Don't be afraid! The secret to a good steak is to get a nice crust, and you can only do that at a high temperature.

❖ Spray the grill grate with nonstick cooking spray. Wearing heavy-duty gloves, place the steaks on the grill with tongs. It is possible flames will appear. This is a good thing. Close the lid and grill the steaks for 5 minutes. Turn over the steaks—it's possible flames will appear again when you do this, so use those gloves and tongs. Grill for 3 minutes longer and begin checking the meat. A probe thermometer will register 135 to 140 degrees for medium-rare. Practice your "palm" technique (see page 45) at the same time.

❖ Remove the steaks to a clean platter and let them stand, covered with foil, for 10 to 15 minutes.

❖ This may seem like a long recipe for grilling a steak but once you get this technique down you can grill a perfect steak every time—no matter the cut.

❖ Serves 2.

Flank Steak ⟩ Grilled ⟨

Flank steak is one of the most affordable cuts of beef and one of the most delicious. The trick is to cook it until it's medium-rare, and cut thin slices across the grain. This makes a juicy, tender piece of meat.

> **1½ pounds flank steak**
> **Grill seasoning (such as McCormick® Grill Mates®**
> **Montreal Steak Seasoning)**
> **Nonstick cooking spray**

❖ Remove the flank steak from the refrigerator and allow it to come to room temperature. Sprinkle the steak liberally with the steak seasoning.

❖ Heat the grill to 500 degrees.

❖ Spray the grill grate with nonstick cooking spray and place the steak on the grill. Close the lid and grill for 5 minutes. Turn over the steak and cook for 3 minutes longer. Test for doneness by using the "palm" method (see page 45) or by inserting a probe thermometer. The thermometer will register 135 degrees for medium-rare.

❖ Remove the steak to a clean platter and let it stand, covered with foil, for 10 to 15 minutes.

❖ Slice the steak thinly across the grain and serve.

❖ Serves 4 to 6.

Hamburgers Grilled

The trick to making a great hamburger is not to handle the meat too much. That's why I use two forks to mix seasonings into the hamburger and then gently form the patties by hand. Ground chuck has the highest fat content of any ground beef and, therefore, makes a better burger. The pat of butter just gilds the lily.

1 pound ground chuck
1 teaspoon salt
½ teaspoon pepper
4 slices chilled butter
Grill seasoning (such as Cavender's®
All Purpose Greek Seasoning)
Nonstick cooking spray

❖ Heat the grill to medium-high, about 400 degrees.

❖ Combine the ground chuck, salt and pepper in a bowl and mix lightly with two forks. Divide the meat into 4 portions and slip a pat of butter into each portion. Gently shape each portion into a patty, making sure the butter is completely enclosed. Make an indentation in the middle of each patty so it's slightly concave to ensure even cooking. Sprinkle with the grill seasoning.

❖ Spray the grill grate with cooking spray and slip the patties onto the grill. Don't press them or the juices will be released. Close the lid; grill for 4 minutes. Turn over the burgers and grill with the lid closed for 3 minutes longer.

❖ Remove the hamburgers to a clean platter and let them stand, covered with foil, for 10 to 15 minutes.

❖ Serve on buttered and grilled hamburger buns (if you think butter is over the top, at least grill the buns—it makes a huge difference).

❖ Serves 4.

Lamb ▶ **Grilled** ◀

Lamb is a much-maligned meat because it is so often cooked improperly. Cook lamb chops to medium-rare and you'll be a convert. They taste like a rich steak. Overcook lamb and it becomes gamey and unpalatable. Be aware, girls, this is one of those recipes where you'll need your heavy gloves and tongs. Lamb contains quite a bit of fat and the fat dripping on the fire will produce flare-ups (and great flavor).

> **2 garlic cloves, minced**
> **1 cup extra-virgin olive oil**
> **Juice of ½ of a lemon**
> **½ teaspoon dried rosemary**
> **4 lamb chops**
> **Nonstick cooking spray**

❖ Combine the garlic, olive oil, lemon juice and rosemary in a flat glass dish large enough to hold the chops; whisk well. Add the lamb chops. Marinate, covered, in the refrigerator for 4 to 6 hours. Drain the lamb chops.

❖ Heat the grill to high, about 500 degrees.

❖ Spray the grill grate with nonstick cooking spray. Grill the lamb chops with the lid closed for 5 minutes. Turn over the chops and grill for 3 minutes longer before testing with a probe thermometer. The probe thermometer will register 140 degrees for medium-rare lamb. (Remember to insert the probe in the thickest part of the meat, not touching the bone.) Practice your "palm" technique (see page 45) at the same time.

❖ Remove the lamb to a clean platter and let it stand, covered with foil, for 10 to 15 minutes.

❖ Serves 2.

Chicken ⟩ Grilled ⟨

Chicken pieces vary in size, so you will have to learn to be intuitive about the timing on this recipe. That's the reason a probe thermometer is so handy—it takes a lot of the guesswork out of judging when the chicken is done. The cornstarch will give your chicken a crispy skin.

1 cup vegetable oil
1/3 cup Worcestershire sauce
Juice of 2 lemons
1 package skin-on chicken pieces (breasts, legs, thighs)
Mayhew's Special Seasoning (see page 32)
Cornstarch
Nonstick cooking spray

❖ Heat the grill to medium, about 350 degrees.

❖ Combine the vegetable oil, Worcestershire sauce and lemon juice in a small bowl and whisk well to make a basting sauce.

❖ Rinse the chicken and pat dry. Sprinkle liberally with Special Seasoning. Sprinkle with cornstarch.

❖ Spray the grill grate with nonstick cooking spray. Place the chicken on the grill and baste it with the lemon juice mixture. Close the lid and grill for about 10 minutes or until the skin releases easily from the grate. Turn over the chicken and baste once more. Insert a probe thermometer in one of the breast pieces, being careful not to touch the bone. Close the lid and grill about 10 minutes longer or to 165 degrees on the thermometer. Remove the breast pieces from the grill. Finish grilling the thighs and legs to 165 degrees on the thermometer.

❖ Remove the chicken to a clean platter and let it stand, covered with foil, for 10 to 15 minutes.

❖ Serves 4.

Boneless Skinless Chicken Breasts

What is more versatile than a chicken breast? Make double the recipe and use the leftovers for chicken fajitas, chicken salad, or a pizza topping. Because the breasts have no skin, keeping them moist can be an issue, but that's where the Italian dressing comes in. It both seasons the breasts and keeps them moist. You can also use brine for this recipe (see page 39).

1 1/2 pounds boneless skinless chicken breasts
1 (8-ounce) bottle Italian dressing
(such as Paul Newman's®)
Mayhew's Special Seasoning (see page 32)
Nonstick cooking spray

❖ Rinse the chicken and pat dry. Combine the chicken pieces and Italian dressing in a heavy-duty gallon plastic bag. Seal the bag and place in a bowl or container to guard against leaks. Marinate the chicken in the refrigerator for up to 4 hours. Drain the chicken and discard the marinade. Pat the chicken dry and place it on a plate. Sprinkle with Special Seasoning.

❖ Heat the grill to medium, about 350 degrees.

❖ Spray the grill grate with nonstick cooking spray. Arrange the chicken breasts on the grate and grill with the lid closed for 7 minutes. Turn over the chicken. Insert the probe thermometer in the thickest part of one of the breasts and grill to 165 degrees.

❖ Remove the chicken to a clean platter and let it stand, covered with foil, for 10 to 15 minutes.

❖ Serves 4.

Turkey Breast ⟩ **Grilled** ⟨

Every so often my grocer offers split turkey breasts at a bargain, and I usually snap up three or four and freeze them. Grilling them is easy and the brine, which adds moisture to the meat, makes them unbelievably juicy. Double this recipe if you want leftovers for Turkey Hot Browns (see page 100) or Creamed Turkey in Pastry Shells (see page 101).

2 quarts water	**1 turkey breast, skin on**
¼ cup each kosher salt and firmly packed dark brown sugar	**Cornstarch**
	Mayhew's Special Seasoning (see page 32)
1 bay leaf	**Nonstick cooking spray**
2 garlic cloves	

❖ Heat the water in a saucepan over medium heat on the stove. Add the kosher salt and stir to dissolve. Add the brown sugar, bay leaf and garlic; stir to dissolve the brown sugar. Cool this brine completely in the saucepan.

❖ Rinse the turkey breast and pat dry. Submerge the turkey breast in the cooled brine and marinate, covered, in the refrigerator for 2 to 3 hours. Remove the breast from the brine and pat dry. Discard the brine.

❖ Heat the grill to medium, about 350 degrees.

❖ Rub the cornstarch into the turkey skin. Spray the turkey breast with nonstick cooking spray and liberally apply the Mayhew's Special Seasoning.

❖ Spray the grill grate with nonstick cooking spray. Place the turkey on the grate, skin side down. Grill with the lid closed for 10 minutes. Turn over the turkey breast and insert a probe thermometer in the thickest part of the turkey breast. Close the grill lid and continue cooking until the turkey reaches 165 degrees internal temperature. Remove the turkey breast to a clean platter and let it stand, covered with foil, for 10 to 15 minutes.

❖ Serves 2 to 3.

Pork Chops **Grilled**

Pork is so lean that it's easy to cook it into shoe leather. To keep the meat moist, use a marinade. You can substitute bone-in pork chops for boneless—they have more flavor because of the bone, but they're not as kid-friendly. You might also brine the chops before grilling.

1 cup apple juice
1/2 cup soy sauce
1 tablespoon honey
4 (1-inch-thick) boneless pork chops
Nonstick cooking spray

❖ Combine the apple juice, soy sauce and honey in a bowl and whisk to blend. Place the pork chops in a heavy-duty gallon bag and pour the apple juice mixture over the chops. Seal the bag and place it in a bowl or container to guard against leaks. Marinate in the refrigerator for up to 3 hours.

❖ Heat the grill to medium, about 350 degrees.

❖ Remove the pork from the marinade. Discard the marinade.

❖ Spray the grill grate with nonstick cooking spray. Grill the pork chops with the lid closed for 5 minutes. Turn over the chops and insert a probe meat thermometer in one of the chops. Continue grilling with the lid closed until the chops reach an internal temperature of 160 degrees.

❖ Remove the pork to a clean platter and let it stand, covered with foil, for 10 to 15 minutes.

❖ Serves 4.

Pork Tenderloin **Grilled**

Pork tenderloin is the jewel of the pig. It's lean and flavorful and easy to cook. Be sure you differentiate between pork tenderloin and pork roast, which is about four times the size of a tenderloin. Most tenderloins come two to a package. Cook both of them and eat them, or use the leftovers in a variety of recipes.

> **I pork tenderloin, about I pound**
> **Mayhew's Special Seasoning (see page 32)**
> **Nonstick cooking spray**

❖ Heat the grill to medium, about 350 degrees.

❖ Trim the silver skin and excess fat from the tenderloin and discard.

❖ Sprinkle the tenderloin liberally with the Special Seasoning.

❖ Spray the grill grate with nonstick cooking spray. Place the tenderloin on the grate and cook with the grill lid closed, turning the tenderloin until it's nicely browned on all sides. Once the tenderloin is browned, cook to 160 degrees on a probe thermometer.

❖ Remove the tenderloin to a clean platter and let it stand, covered with foil, for 10 to 15 minutes.

❖ Serves 2 to 3.

Salmon **Grilled**

I'm using salmon as an example of grilling any fish, because the test for doneness is the same whether it is salmon or tilapia. The finished product should flake easily but still be moist.

1 (16-ounce) piece of skinless salmon
Extra-virgin olive oil
Mayhew's Special Seasoning (see page 32)
Nonstick cooking spray

❖ Heat the grill to medium, about 350 degrees.
❖ Brush the salmon with extra-virgin olive oil and sprinkle with Special Seasoning.
❖ Spray a grill basket with nonstick cooking spray and place the salmon in the basket. Grill the salmon with the lid closed for about 5 minutes on each side.
❖ Remove the salmon to a clean platter and let it stand, covered with foil, for 10 to 15 minutes.
❖ Serves 4.

Hot Tips

Marinate meat in a heavy-duty plastic bag so you can just toss the bag after marinating is complete. Put the bag in a container when you put it in the refrigerator, just in case it leaks.

Appetizers

Chapter Six

I can make a meal out of appetizers, and I confess that I have. Not everything lends itself to the grill and appetizers fall into that category. Most of these recipes do use the grill; a couple of others are just yummy and true favorites of my family and friends.

Grilling appetizers is a great way to use your grill space to maximum efficiency. Put on some Jalapeño Poppers, some Brown Sugar Bacon Bites, and Sausage Stuffed Mushrooms all at the same time. Instant party.

Tender Chicken with Peanut Sauce  **Grilled**

This is a grilled version of the Thai satay, those delicious marinated strips of chicken served with a peanut dipping sauce. Soaking the chicken in buttermilk makes it unbelievably tender.

> **3 boneless skinless chicken breasts**
> **2 cups (about) buttermilk**
> **Cavender's All Purpose Greek Seasoning®**
> **Nonstick cooking spray**

❖ Heat the grill to medium, about 350 degrees.

❖ Trim the chicken breasts of any fat and cut them horizontally into 1-inch strips. Flatten the strips with a meat mallet. Place the flattened strips in a glass dish and add enough buttermilk to cover; make sure each chicken strip is coated in buttermilk. Chill, covered, for up to 3 hours.

❖ Remove the chicken from the buttermilk and wipe off the excess liquid. Sprinkle liberally with the Cavender's® seasoning.

❖ Spray a grill pan with nonstick cooking spray. Arrange the chicken in the grill pan. Grill the strips for about 1 minute per side or until they begin to brown. Or thread the strips onto bamboo skewers that have been soaked in water for 30 minutes, and cook them on the grill for 1 minute per side.

❖ Serve with Peanut Sauce (see next page).

❖ Serves 4.

The Peanut Sauce

 1 tablespoon peanut butter
 1 tablespoon chili sauce
 1 tablespoon soy sauce
 1 tablespoon heavy cream
 1/2 teaspoon hot sauce
 1/2 teaspoon salt
 1/2 teaspoon brown sugar
 1/4 teaspoon curry powder

❖ Combine the peanut butter, chili sauce, soy sauce, cream, hot sauce, salt, brown sugar and curry powder in a small bowl and whisk until well blended.

❖ Serves 4.

Hot Tips

Mix sour cream and salsa in equal parts for a quick sauce for quesadillas or taquitos.

Slice leftover grilled pork tenderloin, and make little sandwiches with frozen yeast rolls and prepared honey mustard.

Cream Cheese Jalapeño Poppers

This savory recipe is probably more suited for adult tastes because of the heat from the jalapeños, but adults need to have a little fun, too!

4 slices bacon
1/2 cup chopped red onion
1/2 cup finely chopped mushrooms
8 ounces cream cheese, softened
1/4 cup shredded Monterey Jack cheese
1/4 cup shredded mozzarella cheese
About 12 large jalapeño peppers
6 slices bacon, cut into halves crosswise
Wooden toothpicks

❖ Bake the bacon on a foil-lined baking sheet at 400 degrees for 20 minutes in the oven. Drain, reserving 1 to 2 tablespoons of the drippings. Cool and crumble the bacon. Spoon the reserved drippings into a medium sauté pan. Sauté the onions and mushrooms in the drippings over medium-high heat on the stove until the mushrooms are browned and the onions are translucent. Cool and set aside.

❖ Heat the grill to medium, about 350 degrees.

❖ Combine the cream cheese, Monterey Jack and mozzarella in a medium bowl. Add the crumbled bacon and mushroom mixture and mix well.

❖ Cut each pepper in half lengthwise; remove the membrane and the seeds. Fill each pepper half with the cream cheese mixture. Wrap a half-strip of raw bacon around each filled pepper and secure with a wooden toothpick.

❖ Grill with the lid open until all the bacon is browned, turning occasionally.

❖ Serves 6 to 8.

Brie and Apricot Crostini   **Grilled**

Crostini are small, thin slices of toasted bread, which are usually brushed with olive oil and topped with…anything! These simple appetizers pack a lot of flavor. Cheese and fruit are always a good combination and here, they're dynamite.

1 **French baguette**
   Extra-virgin olive oil
   Salt
1 **small round Brie cheese**
   Apricot preserves

❖ Heat the grill to medium-high, about 400 degrees.

❖ Cut the baguette into ¼-inch slices. Brush both sides of each slice with olive oil and sprinkle with salt. Grill the slices with the lid open for about 1 minute on each side until the bread is slightly charred. Remove to a plate and let stand until cool.

❖ Cut the Brie cheese into thin slices. Top each crostini with a slice of Brie and a dab of apricot preserves.

❖ Yields about 20 crostini.

Hot Tips

Frozen green beans can go directly into a sauté pan on the stove with some extra-virgin olive oil over medium-high heat. Add slices of fresh garlic when the beans are almost done, when they start to brown a little bit.

Pepper Jelly Cream Cheese Crostini

Cream cheese and pepper jelly are a classic combination usually served with crackers, but they're also great on bread. Look for pepper jelly in the same section of the supermarket where regular jelly is sold.

1 French baguette
 Extra-virgin olive oil
 Salt
 Cream cheese
1 jar green or red pepper jelly

❖ Heat the grill to medium-high, about 400 degrees.

❖ Cut the bread into 1/4-inch slices. Brush the slices with olive oil and sprinkle with salt. Grill each side for about 1 minute or until slightly charred. Remove to a plate and cool.

❖ Spread each slice with cream cheese and top with pepper jelly.

❖ Yields about 20 crostini.

Hot Tips

When you buy a grill, always buy the best you can afford. A high-quality grill can last for years, and you won't remember how much it cost.

Brown Sugar Bacon Bites ⟩ Grilled ⟨

Brown sugar and bacon are a classic combination—sweet and salty. If you want to leave out the mushrooms, you can grill the sugar-coated bacon by itself and create one of the great treats of all time—Pig Candy. (For those who don't know, Pig Candy is a snack made out of smoky, thick-cut bacon baked with lots and lots of brown sugar.)

> **12 slices bacon**
> **Brown sugar**
> **24 fresh button mushroom caps, cleaned,**
> **stems removed**
> **Nonstick cooking spray**

❖ Cut the bacon slices into halves crosswise and bring to room temperature.

❖ Heat ¹⁄₂ of the grill to medium, about 350 degrees. If you're using a charcoal grill, bank the coals to one side and light them; you will use the cooler portion of the grate.

❖ Dust one side of each bacon piece with brown sugar. Wrap a half-strip of bacon around each mushroom cap, brown sugar side out, and secure with a wooden toothpick.

❖ Spray a grill pan with nonstick cooking oil. Arrange the wrapped mushrooms in the grill pan. Grill over indirect heat for about 10 minutes or until bacon is browned evenly on all sides, turning occasionally.

❖ Yields 24 bacon bites.

Sausage-Stuffed Mushrooms  **Grilled**

Stuffed mushrooms are easy to make and, at least at my house, there are never leftovers! You can stuff mushrooms with anything—breadcrumbs, hamburger, whatever your kids like. But this is how we like them best.

> **8 ounces bulk pork sausage**
> **3 tablespoons chopped red onion**
> **¾ cup shredded cheese**
> **½ cup seasoned breadcrumbs**
> **1 pound whole white mushrooms**
> **¼ cup olive oil**
> **Additional cheese**

❖ Heat ½ of the grill to medium-high, about 400 degrees. If you're using a charcoal grill, bank the coals to one side and light them.

❖ Cook the sausage in a heavy skillet over medium heat on the stove until it is cooked through and beginning to brown; break up the meat as much as possible. Spoon the sausage into a medium bowl lined with paper towels, allowing the drippings to remain in the skillet.

❖ Sauté the onion in the sausage drippings over medium-low heat on the stove for 10 minutes or until translucent. Remove the paper towels from the bowl and stir the sautéed onions into the sausage. Add the ¾ cup shredded cheese and breadcrumbs; mix well.

❖ Remove the stems from the mushrooms and brush off any dirt on the caps with a damp paper towel. Brush the outside of the mushroom caps with olive oil and fill the caps with the sausage mixture. Top with additional cheese.

❖ Place the mushrooms in a grill basket on the unlit part of the grill. Close the lid and grill for about 10 minutes or until the cheese is melted and the mushrooms are brown.

❖ Yields about 18 pieces.

Eggplant Caviar **Grilled**

Kids may not like eggplant unadorned, but with this combination of the herbs, garlic, and tomato, the humble eggplant becomes something special.

1 **large eggplant**
   Nonstick cooking spray
1 **medium onion, chopped**
2 **garlic cloves, minced**
2 **tablespoons extra-virgin olive oil**
2 **tomatoes, seeded and chopped**
1 **teaspoon dried basil**
1 **teaspoon dried thyme**
1 **cup tomato sauce**
   Salt and pepper to taste

❖ Heat the grill to medium, about 350 degrees.

❖ Peel the eggplant and slice into 1/2-inch rounds. Salt the eggplant rounds and let them drain on paper towels for 30 minutes to release the bitterness.

❖ Spray a grill pan with oil and place the eggplant slices in the pan. Grill with the lid closed for about 3 minutes per side. Remove the eggplant slices from the grill and let stand until cool. Chop into chunks.

❖ Sauté the onion and garlic in the olive oil in a heavy skillet over medium-low heat on the stove for about 5 minutes. Stir in the tomatoes, basil, thyme, tomato sauce and eggplant. Bring to a boil. Reduce heat and simmer for about 30 minutes or until the mixture becomes very thick. Season with salt and pepper.

❖ Cool to lukewarm. Chill, covered, for at least 2 hours. Serve as a spread with toast points or party rye bread.

❖ Yields about 2 cups.

Grilled Pita Wedges **Grilled**

The dipping sauce for these grilled pitas is traditionally called tzatziki sauce. You can also use it on homemade gyros.

> 1 tablespoon extra-virgin olive oil
> 4 whole pita breads
> Dried oregano
> Salt to taste

❖ Heat the grill to medium-high, about 400 degrees.

❖ Brush both sides of each pita bread lightly with olive oil. Sprinkle with oregano and salt. Grill both sides on the open grill until lightly charred. Cut into wedges and serve with Greek Dipping Sauce (see below).

❖ Serves 16 as appetizers.

Greek Dipping Sauce

> 1 pint plain yogurt
> 1 small cucumber, peeled and seeded
> 2 small garlic cloves or 1 large garlic clove, minced
> 1 tablespoon extra-virgin olive oil

❖ Grate the cucumber and remove the moisture by squeezing the grated cucumber over a bowl. Mix together the yogurt, cucumber, garlic and olive oil in a small bowl. Chill for at least 1 hour.

Grilled Cocktail Weenie Kabobs

No time? No problem. These kabobs are easy to make and sure to be a hit, particularly with kids.

1 pound cocktail franks
8 ounces Cheddar cheese, cut into 1-inch cubes

❖ Heat the grill to medium-high, about 400 degrees.
❖ Place the cocktail franks in the grill basket and grill with the lid closed until the franks are nicely browned, turning frequently. Cool slightly.
❖ Spear the franks and the cheese cubes alternately on wooden skewers that have been cut in half for easy handling.
❖ Serve with Barbecue Dipping Sauce (see page 33).
❖ Yields about 20 half-skewers.

Grilled Vegetable Spread

Leftover marinated grilled vegetables can make a terrific spread. The vegetables already have a great flavor from the marinade and the grill, so you don't need to add other seasonings.

1 cup Marinated Grilled Vegetables (see page 145)
4 ounces cream cheese, softened
4 ounces goat cheese, softened

❖ Place the vegetables in a food processor container and process until minced.
❖ Combine the vegetables with the cream cheese and goat cheese in a medium bowl and mix well. Chill, covered, for at least 1 hour. Serve with crackers or bagel crisps.
❖ Yields about 2 cups.

Moo-Shu Pork Won Tons

I promise this will be a hit at your next party. The easiest way to mince the mushrooms, water chestnuts, and pork tenderloin is in a food processor. You can get the kids to help prepare this by letting them fold the won tons.

1 tablespoon vegetable oil
1 teaspoon dark sesame oil
1/2 cup minced mushrooms
1/3 cup minced water chestnuts
2 cups shredded cabbage
1 teaspoon each minced garlic and minced fresh gingerroot
1 cup minced grilled pork tenderloin
3 teaspoons hoisin sauce
2 teaspoons soy sauce
Won ton wrappers
Vegetable oil for deep-frying

❖ Heat the 1 tablespoon vegetable oil and the sesame oil in a skillet over medium-high heat on the stove. Sauté the mushrooms, water chestnuts and cabbage in the hot oil for about 10 minutes or until the cabbage is translucent and beginning to brown. Add the garlic and gingerroot to the cabbage mixture and sauté for 30 seconds to 1 minute longer. Stir in the pork and heat through. Stir in the hoisin sauce and soy sauce. Spoon the pork mixture into a bowl and let stand until completely cool.

❖ Following package directions, place a scant teaspoon of the pork mixture in the center of each won ton wrapper. Bring the corners of each won ton wrapper together; seal with water.

❖ Heat 2 inches of oil to 375 degrees in a deep saucepan, using a probe thermometer to check the temperature. Fry the won tons for about 30 seconds per side or until nicely browned. Drain the won tons on paper towels and serve with Asian Dipping Sauce (see page 34).

❖ Yields about 30 won tons.

Low-Country Crab Dip

The "low-country" refers to coastal South Carolina, where the crab is sweet and this dip is commonly served. You really don't want canned crab meat for this, so splurge and buy the crab in the refrigerated case of your grocer's seafood department.

1 cup mayonnaise	1/4 cup French dressing
1 cup crab meat	2 tablespoons snipped chives
1/2 cup shredded Cheddar cheese	3 slices bacon
1 tablespoon creamy horseradish	

❖ Combine the mayonnaise, crab meat, Cheddar cheese, horseradish and French dressing in a medium bowl; mix well. Spoon into a decorative bowl and sprinkle with the chives.

❖ Chill, covered, for at least 1 hour. Serve with buttery crackers.

❖ Yields about 2 cups.

Deviled Ham Dip

My mother-in-law, Susan Harbin, throws the best parties in the universe. One of her most-requested recipes is this simple dip. She always serves it with Fritos' Scoops®. This is one the kids can mix up by themselves.

1 (4-ounce) can deviled ham (such as Underwood®)
1 cup sour cream

❖ Combine the ham and the sour cream in a bowl and mix well. Chill, covered, for at least 1 hour. Serve with Scoops® or the chip of your choice.

❖ Yields 1 1/2 cups.

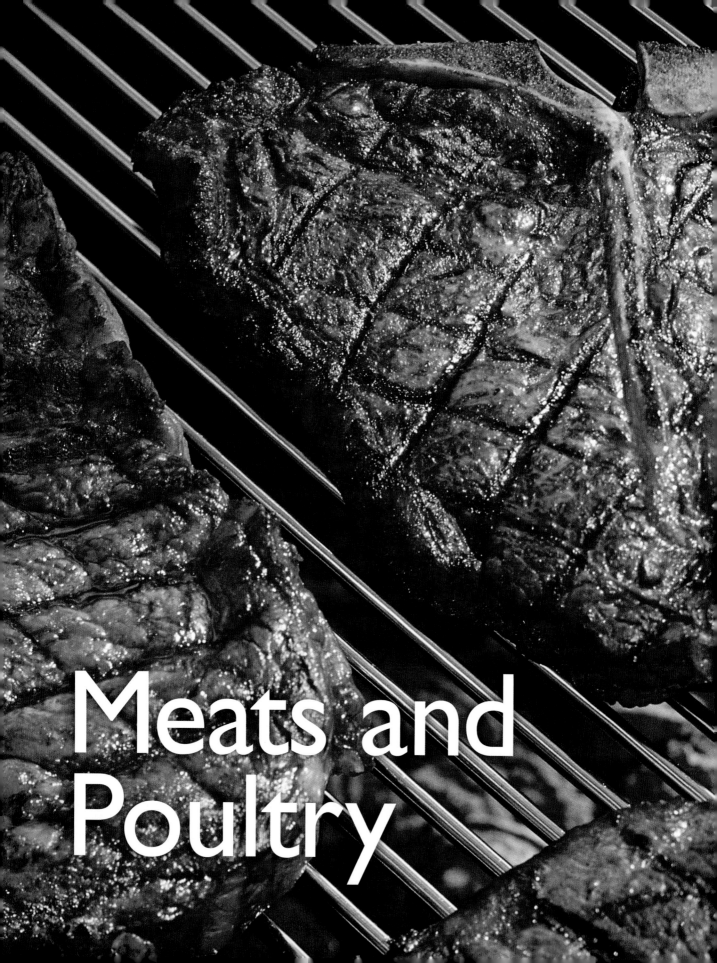

Meats and Poultry

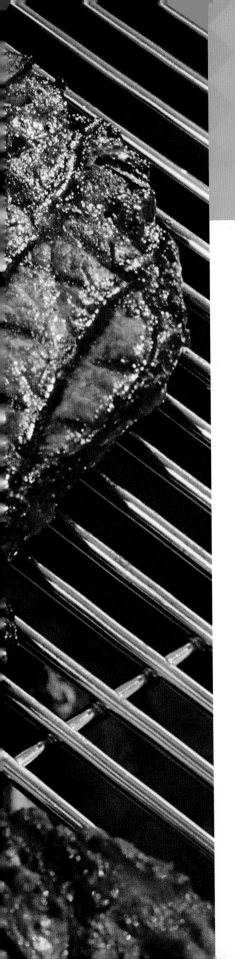

The aroma of a juicy steak, the perfume of crispy chicken skin, or the mahogany sheen of a perfectly grilled pork tenderloin—this is why we grill.

But there are tricks of the trade regarding various cuts and types of meat and poultry. The first thing to remember is that the recipes in this book are really just guidelines. If a recipe calls for a 1-inch steak and the steak you have is a little thicker, you'll just have to adjust the cooking time a bit. No two cooks will make the same recipe the same way. And that's the fun of it.

The Art of Grilling Meats and Poultry

When you put your meat on the grill, close the lid and leave it there for at least 5 minutes. When the meat is ready to turn, it will naturally and easily release from the grill grates. The best advice I got when I started grilling was to stop fussing with the meat and just let it cook without constantly opening the grill lid and turning the meat over.

Before I give you recipes, here is a primer on the most popular cuts of meat and poultry you'll cook on the grill. And be sure to check the Master Recipes chapter for the most basic ways to cook meat and poultry, as well as other helpful hints.

Beef

Nothing sizzles like a steak on the grill. It is the essence of the barbecue. But not all steaks are created equal.

Any kind of steak does well on the grill—**filet mignon, porterhouse, T-bone, ribeye, flank, skirt, and porterhouse.** With any steak, you want to get the grill as hot as you can. Most gas grills won't go beyond 650 degrees, but some charcoal grills can reach temperatures approaching 800 degrees. The idea is to sear in the flavor and juices of the meat by, in essence, sealing the top and bottom.

Flank and skirt steak are the unappreciated workhorses in the steak family. They are affordable and delicious, provided you cook them to medium-rare and slice them thinly across the grain. Beef cuts that require slow cooking, such as round steak, are not good choices for the grill.

There are different ways to test meat for doneness, but by far the most precise for beginning grillers is a probe thermometer. A probe thermometer has a digital readout that will tell you the precise internal temperature of the meat. These thermometers are available at houseware stores and establishments that sell grilling equipment.

You will think the probe thermometers are ridiculously expensive and will be tempted to buy a cheap meat thermometer. Resist temptation and get the probe. It will last a long time, and it works every time. The temperature will register between 135 and 140 degrees for medium-rare.

The other method—and it only works for beef—is the "palm" method. It's what I use exclusively now to achieve the medium-rare steaks my family loves.

The palm method: Flex your thumb and feel the texture of the muscle right below the thumb. It feels like a soft tennis ball. That's medium-rare.

When you're grilling a steak, use the "palm" method to test for doneness after you've flipped the steak and have cooked it for another 2 to 3 minutes. Open the lid and poke the meat at its thickest point with your finger to see if it feels like a soft tennis ball. If the meat is too soft, give the steak another couple of minutes and check it again.

The first time you do this, you may not get it right, but as you cook more and more steaks, you'll get perfectly medium-rare beef every time. Here's your back-up plan for that first time out: Take the steak off the grill and cut into it a little. If it's too rare, throw it in the microwave for 30-second increments until you have the desired result. (By the way, girls, except for those first trial runs when you're getting your technique down, don't ever pierce a piece of meat with a fork or knife. That lets the juices run out, and juices are what make a steak, well, juicy.)

I like beef medium-rare, which means an internal temperature of 145 degrees F for steak. The only safe internal temperature for ground beef is done, and that means 160 degrees F.

Poultry

Chicken is surely the most popular item for the grill. There's nothing like the crispy exterior and juicy interior of a well-grilled piece of chicken.

Chicken is best on the grill with the skin on and the bone in. The bone helps the chicken retain moisture and flavor. You can go crazy with the science of cooking both dark and white meat because they're cooked for different times. But here's what I do to simplify things.

Hot Tips

Always wash platters with hot water and soap after they've held uncooked meat, poultry, or seafood.

Put a probe thermometer in the thickest part of a chicken breast but not touching the bone. Do this after you've grilled the chicken on one side and turned it over. When the temperature reaches 165 degrees, take off the white meat and put the probe in the dark meat. When it reaches 165, remove it from the grill.

Chicken wings are a great way to begin your grilling career because they are very hard to mess up. Their high skin-to-meat ratio means that wings have a built in insulator against over-cooking.

Turkey is underappreciated on the grill. As a working mother, I'm not a big fan of cooking a whole turkey on the grill, although the results are delicious. But my grocer occasionally sells half turkey breasts, and I stock up when they're available and freeze them. Cooking a half turkey breast is just like grilling a chicken breast only bigger. If you grill more than one, you'll have leftovers to make Turkey Hot Browns (see page 100) and the best turkey sandwiches around.

Brining is a good option for poultry. Brine is simply a mixture of water, salt, and sugar. (See page 39.) You can add other flavors to it such as peppercorns, various herbs, and flavored liquids such as apple juice. The brine infuses the chicken with extra moisture, which is worth it especially for boneless, skinless chicken breasts. All you do is mix the brine up over medium heat on the stove so the sugar and salt dissolve. Then cool it before using—very important for sanitary reasons because you don't want the warm brine coming in contact with raw meat thereby creating bacteria. I usually stick the brine in the freezer to speed the cooling process. When the brine is cool, immerse the chicken pieces in it and refrigerate for a couple of hours.

A trick I picked up from my grilling friends is to use cornstarch on the skin when I'm grilling chicken or turkey. It makes the skin crispy. Just dust it on and rub it in—the cornstarch doesn't leave any flavor.

The only safe internal temperature for poultry is done, which means 165 degrees F for whole or parts, and 170 degrees F for ground poultry.

Pork

Today, pigs are bred to be very lean. On the health front, that's a good thing. On the flavor front, it's not so great. So you have to help Mr. Piggy along the way to get a flavorful result.

Pork tenderloin is the easiest cut of pork to grill and, done properly, will come out tender and flavorful. The tenderloin must be trimmed of its silver skin before grilling—it's tough and nothing will tenderize it. (When you look at the pork loin, you'll see a white piece of shiny skin. That's the silver skin.)

Whole pieces of pork (as opposed to ground pork) can be cooked until the center still has a blush of pink in it. Tenderloins are so tender that even if you overcook them, they'll still taste great.

Pork chops need more attention. To make sure they turn out juicy, you will want to brine them just as you do for boneless, skinless chicken breasts. Pork can stand a little more brining than chicken can—up to 12 hours. I usually try for about 4 hours or however long I have from the time I pick my son up from school and the time when I ring the dinner bell.

Pork loin roasts are much better if they're brined for up to 24 hours before cooking. It's very difficult to get a tender piece of pork loin when grilling unless it has been brined.

These days it is perfectly safe to eat pork that is still a little rosy in the center—try it and see the difference between shoe leather pork and properly cooked pork. *Cook pork chops, loins, tenderloins, and ground pork to an internal temperature of 160 degrees.*

Ribs are one of my family's favorites. You'll find two types of ribs in your grocer's meat case—baby backs and spareribs. The essential difference is that they come from different parts of the pig—spareribs come from the bottom of the hog and baby backs come from the top half. Baby backs are more tender but less meaty.

For either baby back ribs or spareribs, you will want to remove the membrane on the back of the ribs before cooking. To do this, insert your finger under the membrane in the middle of the rack of ribs. Once you loosen the membrane, take a paper towel and pull it off. After you get the hang of this, you will look extremely professional just carrying off this one little trick.

My personal feeling is that it's very hard to cook a good rib on a gas grill. I have both gas and charcoal grills, and I always choose charcoal for ribs. To get a good smoky flavor to your ribs, you have to introduce wood and it's just easier in a charcoal grill.

Lamb

In my book, the only cuts of lamb that work well on the grill are **lamb chops** and **ground lamb burgers.** Lamb chops are usually cut about 3 inches thick and come with a fair amount of fat. Be wary as you grill the chops because the fat will produce a significant flame as it drips on the charcoal or gas flame. But that also gives the chop a rich, smoky flavor. *Grill lamb chops to an internal temperature of 145 degrees; burgers to 160 degrees.*

Hamburgers and Hot Dogs

Busy moms will end up grilling hamburgers and hot dogs more than any other meat. They're quick and easy. But all ground beef is not created equal and the same holds true for hot dogs.

Your supermarket carries several cuts of **ground beef.** Ground beef that is labeled chuck, sirloin, or round means that the meat comes from that particular place on the cow. Actually, ground hamburger can come from any part of the cow except organ meats.

The rule of thumb for hamburgers is to get the ground beef that has the most fat in it because fat equals flavor. So the winner here is ground chuck, because it is 15 to 20 percent fat. Ground round has 10 to 15 percent fat and ground sirloin has 8 to 10 percent fat.

The trick to making a really great hamburger is to handle the meat gently. If you pat those burgers out to within an inch of their meaty lives, they'll be dense and dry. I always use two forks to toss the meat with whatever seasonings I add and then gently form them into patties. It's kind of like making biscuits; the more you handle the dough, the tougher the biscuit.

Hot dogs are already cooked mild sausages that can be made of beef, pork, or a combination of the two. For my money, beef hot dogs are the way to go.

Hot dogs also come with or without casings. Actually all hot dogs come in to the world with a casing. The ones sold in the grocery store without were produced using a plastic casing that is removed before the product is packaged.

Natural hot dog casings are made from the small intestines of sheep. They give the dog a snap when you bite it and make the release of juices and flavor more intense. At our house, we only eat hot dogs with natural casings. Try a comparison of the two and decide which you think are more flavorful.

Marinated Filet Mignon ⟫ Grilled ⟪

Marinating filet mignon gives it a depth of flavor.

¹/₂ cup olive oil
¹/₄ cup red wine
2 tablespoons Worcestershire sauce
4 (6-ounce) filet mignons, about 1¹/₂ inches thick
Grill seasoning (such as McCormick® Grill Mates®
Montreal Steak Seasoning)
Nonstick cooking spray

❖ Combine the olive oil, red wine and Worcestershire sauce in a small bowl and whisk well. Pour into a shallow glass dish and add the steaks. Marinate, covered, in the refrigerator for 1 to 2 hours, turning occasionally.

❖ Heat the grill to high, about 500 degrees.

❖ Spray the grill grate with nonstick cooking spray. Remove the steaks from the marinade. Sprinkle grill seasoning liberally over both sides, and place the steaks on the grill.

❖ Grill the filets for 5 minutes with the lid down. Turn over the filets and grill for about 4 minutes longer before testing for doneness.

❖ If you use a probe thermometer, it should register 135 to 140 degrees for medium-rare. Or use the "palm" method (see page 45).

❖ Remove the steaks to a clean platter and let them stand, covered with foil, for 10 to 15 minutes.

❖ Serves 4.

Beef Shish Kabob   Grilled

This is the quintessential outdoor recipe. Kabob pieces are small enough that, when the meat is nicely charred, they're done. But if you're not sure, just remove one of the pieces and cut into it to check—this is the only time I'll recommend cutting a steak to see if it's done!

2 pounds beef tenderloin, sirloin or other high-end steak
1 recipe Red Wine Marinade (see page 37)
1 pound button mushrooms, stems removed
1 large onion, cut in pieces for skewering
1 green bell pepper, cored, seeded, cut in pieces
for skewering
Salt and pepper to taste

❖ Cut the beef into 1½-inch cubes. Combine the beef, marinade, mushrooms, onion and bell pepper in a heavy-duty plastic bag. Seal the bag and place it in a container to guard against leaks. Chill for 6 to 12 hours.

❖ Heat the grill to medium-high, about 400 degrees.

❖ Remove the meat and the vegetables from the marinade, and spear on metal skewers or bamboo skewers that have been soaked in water for 30 minutes. Season with salt and pepper.

❖ Grill the kabobs with the lid open on all sides until nicely charred.

❖ Remove the kabobs to a clean platter and let them stand, covered with foil, for 10 to 15 minutes.

❖ Serves 4.

Marinated Flank Steak

Flank steak is one of the most affordable cuts of beef and one of the most delicious. The trick to grilling it is to cook it until it's medium-rare. Then cut thin slices across the grain, and you have a juicy, tender piece of meat. Marinating the meat for up to 24 hours before you grill it makes the steak even more tender.

> 1 ½ **cups beer**
> 3 **green onions, finely chopped**
> ⅓ **cup olive oil**
> 3 **tablespoons soy sauce**
> 2 **tablespoons sugar**
> 2 **large garlic cloves, minced**
> 1 **teaspoon salt**
> 1 ½ **pounds flank steak**

❖ Combine the beer, green onions, olive oil, soy sauce, sugar, garlic and salt in a bowl and whisk well. Place the beer mixture and steak in a heavy-duty plastic bag. Seal tightly and place in a container to guard against leaks. Marinate in the refrigerator for up to 24 hours. (Moms, don't sweat it if the steak marinates for as few as 10 hours or as many as 30. It will still be good.)

❖ Heat the grill to high, about 500 degrees.

❖ Remove the steak from the refrigerator and let it come to room temperature.

❖ Spray the grill grate with nonstick cooking spray. Remove the meat from the plastic bag with tongs and place it on the grill. Grill with the lid closed for 5 minutes. Turn over the steak and cook for 3 minutes before testing for doneness. If you use a probe thermometer, it should register 135 to 140 degrees for medium-rare. Or use the "palm" method (see page 45).

❖ Remove the steak to a clean platter and let it stand, covered with foil, for 10 to 15 minutes.

❖ Slice thinly across the grain and serve.

❖ Serves 4 to 6.

Garlic Herb Steak Panini **Grilled**

Skirt steak is a sort of kissing cousin to flank steak. It's most often used in fajitas. In fact, you can marinate and grill the skirt steak for these sandwiches or just warm up some tortillas and make fajitas instead.

> 1/2 **cup vegetable oil**
> **Juice of 1 lemon**
> 2 **tablespoons Worcestershire sauce**
> 1 **teaspoon Italian herbs**
> **Salt and pepper to taste**
> 1 **pound skirt steak**
> 2 **tablespoons vegetable oil**
> 8 **ounces button mushrooms, sliced**
> **Salt and pepper to taste**
> 1/4 **cup red wine**
> 2 **orange bell peppers, cored, sliced lengthwise**
> **Nonstick cooking spray**
> 2 **(8-ounce) French baguettes**
> **Garlic-herb cheese spread (such as Alouette® brand)**
> 8 to10 **baby spinach leaves**

❖ Combine the 1/2 cup vegetable oil, lemon juice, Worcestershire sauce and Italian herbs in a small bowl and whisk well. Whisk in salt and pepper. Put the vegetable oil mixture and the steak in a heavy-duty gallon plastic bag; seal and place in a bowl or container to guard against leaks. Marinate in the refrigerator for 4 to 24 hours.

❖ Heat the 2 tablespoons vegetable oil in a skillet over medium-high heat on the stove. Add the mushrooms, salt and pepper. Sauté the mushrooms for 5 to 10 minutes or until they begin to brown. Stir in the red wine. Sauté for 5 minutes longer or until the moisture is gone and mushrooms are nicely browned.

❖ Heat the grill to high, about 500 degrees.

❖ Grill the bell pepper slices until lightly charred.

❖ Spray the grill grate with nonstick cooking spray. Remove the meat from the marinade bag with tongs and place it on the grill. Grill with the lid closed for 5 minutes. Turn over the steak and grill for 3 minutes longer before testing for doneness. If you use a probe thermometer, it should register 135 to 140 degrees for medium-rare; see page 45 for other temperatures. Or use the "palm" method (see page 45).

❖ Remove the steak to a platter and let it stand, covered with foil, for 10 to 15 minutes. Cut the steak across the grain into thin slices.

❖ Reduce the grill heat to low. Cut the ends off each baguette and cut each baguette crosswise into 2 pieces. Slice the bread pieces lengthwise to make enough slices for 4 sandwiches. Spread the cut sides with garlic-herb spread. Lay 8 to 10 slices of skirt steak lengthwise over each of 2 bread slices. Layer slices of orange pepper, mushrooms and baby spinach over the meat. Top with the remaining bread slices and press to compress the sandwiches.

❖ Return the sandwiches to the grill and press with a heavy pan. (You can also use a Panini maker to press the sandwiches.) Grill with the lid open until one side is crisp. Turn over the sandwiches and grill the other side.

❖ Serves 4.

Southern Burgers   Grilled

Hamburgers and coleslaw are a combination you see frequently in the South. The creaminess of the coleslaw complements the richness of the burger.

> **1 pound ground chuck**
> **1 teaspoon salt**
> **1/2 teaspoon pepper**
> **4 slices chilled butter**
> **Grill seasoning (such as McCormick® Grill Mates®**
> **Montreal Steak Seasoning)**
> **Nonstick cooking spray**
> **4 slices Cheddar cheese**
> **Prepared coleslaw**
> **Your favorite barbecue sauce**
> **4 hamburger buns**

❖ Heat the grill to medium-high, about 400 degrees.

❖ Combine the ground chuck, salt and pepper in a bowl and mix lightly with two forks. Divide the meat into 4 portions and slip a pat of butter into each portion. Gently shape each portion into a patty, making sure the butter is completely enclosed. Make an indentation in the middle of each patty so it's slightly concave to ensure even cooking. Sprinkle with the grill seasoning.

❖ Spray the grill grate with nonstick cooking spray. Slip the patties on the grate and grill with the lid closed for 4 minutes. (Do not press the patties, or the juices will be released). Turn over the burgers and grill with the lid closed for 3 minutes longer.

❖ Top each burger with a slice of cheese, close the lid and grill for about 30 seconds or until the cheese is melted. Remove the burgers from the grill.

❖ Butter and grill 4 hamburger buns. Assemble the burgers using the coleslaw and the barbecue sauce as condiments.

❖ Serves 4.

Meatloaf Burger [Grilled]

The name says it all.

1/4	cup vegetable oil	1 1/2	teaspoons salt
1	cup chopped green bell pepper	3/4	teaspoon pepper
1	cup plus 2 tablespoons chopped yellow onion	1/2	cup Italian breadcrumbs
			Nonstick cooking spray
1	(8-ounce) can tomato sauce	4	slices sharp Cheddar cheese
2	tablespoons Worcestershire sauce	4	potato hamburger rolls
			Butter
1 1/2	pounds ground chuck		Mayonnaise
			Iceberg lettuce

❖ Heat the vegetable oil in a heavy sauté pan over medium-low heat on the stove. Sauté the bell pepper and the onion in the hot oil until translucent. Set aside to cool completely.

❖ Combine the onion mixture, tomato sauce, Worcestershire sauce, ground chuck, salt, pepper and Italian breadcrumbs in a large bowl; mix gently with 2 forks. Shape loosely into 4 patties.

❖ Heat the grill to medium-high, about 400 degrees.

❖ Spray the grill grate with nonstick cooking spray. Slip the patties onto the grate and grill with the lid closed for 4 minutes. (Do not press the patties or the juices will be released). Turn over the burgers and grill with the lid closed for 3 minutes longer.

❖ Top each burger with a slice of cheese, close the lid and grill for about 30 seconds or until the cheese is melted. Remove the burgers from the grill.

❖ Split the potato hamburger rolls and butter them. Grill the rolls until lightly toasted. Spread the mayonnaise over the rolls. Fill the rolls with the burgers and lettuce.

❖ Serves 4.

Grilled Meatloaf ➤ **Grilled**

My husband says the only reason that I make meatloaf is so I can have meatloaf sandwiches the next day. He's right. (Perfect meatloaf sandwich: meatloaf, mayonnaise, salt, pepper, lettuce and soft bread.) If your grocer doesn't carry meatloaf mix (which is ground beef mixed with ground pork), you can substitute ground beef. Panko breadcrumbs are coarser than regular ones and can be found in the Asian section of your supermarket.

1½ pounds (about) meatloaf mix	1 cup Panko breadcrumbs
¼ cup chopped red onion	1½ teaspoons salt
¼ cup chopped red bell pepper	½ teaspoon black pepper
2 eggs, beaten	½ teaspoon garlic powder
1 (8-ounce) can tomato sauce	1 teaspoon dried oregano
1 tablespoon Worcestershire sauce	2 slices (or more) bread
	Your favorite barbecue sauce

❖ Heat the grill to medium, about 350 degrees.

❖ Combine the meatloaf mix, red onion, bell pepper, eggs, tomato sauce, Worcestershire sauce, breadcrumbs, salt, pepper, garlic powder and oregano in a large bowl; clean hands are your best tools here.

❖ Line a baking pan with foil and place the bread slices in the pan to soak up excess grease as the meatloaf cooks. Place a wire rack (the kind you would use to cool cookies) over the top of the pan. Shape the meat mixture into a loaf and place it on the wire rack.

❖ Place the pan on the grill grate and insert a probe thermometer about halfway into the meatloaf. Grill with the lid closed until the meatloaf reaches an internal temperature of 160 degrees. Check about halfway through and cover the meatloaf with foil if it is getting too brown on top. Baste the meatloaf with barbecue sauce about 10 minutes before the end of cooking time.

❖ Cool the meatloaf slightly and remove to a serving plate. Discard the bread slices.

❖ Serves 4 to 6.

Lamb Burgers **Grilled**

These open-faced burgers are terrific with Greek Dipping Sauce (see page 66).

> 1 **pound ground lamb**
> 1/4 **cup minced red onion**
> 1/2 **cup minced parsley**
> 2 **garlic cloves, minced**
> 1 **teaspoon salt**
> 1/2 **teaspoon freshly ground black pepper**
> **Nonstick cooking spray**
> 4 **slices rustic bread**
> **Extra-virgin olive oil**

❖ Heat the grill to medium-high, about 400 degrees.

❖ Combine the lamb, red onion, parsley, garlic, salt and pepper in a medium bowl and mix well. Shape into 4 patties.

❖ Spray the grill grate with nonstick cooking spray. Grill the patties with the lid closed for 4 minutes. Turn over the patties and grill with the lid closed for 3 minutes longer or until they are nicely browned on both sides. Remove the patties to a clean platter and let them stand, covered with foil, for 10 minutes.

❖ Brush both sides of each bread slice with olive oil and sprinkle with additional salt. Grill the oiled bread until slightly charred on both sides.

❖ Serve the lamb patties, topped with Greek Dipping Sauce (see page 66), on the grilled bread.

❖ Serves 4.

Pork Tenderloin with Apricot Glaze

Pork tenderloin is my go-to meat on a busy weeknight because it cooks fast and is always delicious. Leftover pork tenderloin is wonderful sliced on yeast rolls with honey mustard.

2 pork tenderloins
¼ cup soy sauce
1 cup apple juice
1 teaspoon chopped fresh
    gingerroot

1 garlic clove, chopped
Salt and pepper to taste
Nonstick cooking spray
½ cup apricot jam
2 teaspoons Dijon mustard

❖ Trim the silver skin and excess fat from the tenderloins and discard.

❖ Combine the soy sauce, apple juice, gingerroot and garlic in a bowl and whisk well. Place the apple juice mixture and tenderloin in a heavy-duty plastic bag. Seal tightly, pressing out the air, and place in a container to guard against leaks. Marinate in the refrigerator for 2 to 12 hours, turning the bag periodically.

❖ Heat the grill to medium, about 350 degrees.

❖ Spray the grill grate with nonstick cooking spray. Remove the tenderloins from the marinade, brushing off any bits of garlic and gingerroot. Season the tenderloins with salt and pepper. Grill the tenderloins with the lid closed, turning as necessary until they are nicely browned on both sides. Once the tenderloins are browned, cook them to an internal temperature of 160 degrees on a probe thermometer.

❖ Remove the tenderloins to a clean platter and let them stand, covered with foil, for 10 minutes.

❖ Melt the apricot jam in a small saucepan over low heat on the stove. Add the Dijon mustard and mix well. Brush the apricot mixture over the tenderloins and serve.

❖ Note: Steven Raichlen's Island Spice Barbecue Rub® is really great as a substitute for salt and pepper in this recipe.

❖ Serves 4.

Glazed Pork Tenderloin Filets

Just as you can slice beef tenderloin and get filet mignon, you can slice pork tenderloin and get incredibly tender pork steaks. Hoisin sauce is the Chinese version of ketchup. You can find it in the Asian section of your supermarket.

2 pork tenderloins
Salt and pepper to taste
4 tablespoons hoisin sauce
2 tablespoons apple juice
2 teaspoons Dijon mustard
Nonstick cooking spray

❖ Heat the grill to medium, about 350 degrees.

❖ Trim the silver skin and excess fat from the tenderloins and discard. Cut the tenderloins into 1-inch-thick slices. Press down on each slice to flatten it a little. Season with salt and pepper.

❖ Combine the hoisin sauce, apple juice and Dijon mustard in a small bowl and mix well. Brush the tops of the tenderloin slices with the hoisin sauce mixture.

❖ Spray the grill grate with nonstick cooking spray and place the tenderloin slices on the grill, sauce side down. Brush the other side of the tenderloin slices with the sauce and grill with the lid closed for 3 minutes. Turn over the tenderloin slices and grill with the lid closed for 2 minutes longer.

❖ Remove the tenderloin slices to a clean platter and let them stand, covered with foil, for 10 minutes.

❖ Brush the slices with additional sauce and serve.

❖ Serves 4.

Sesame Ginger Pork Kabobs ⟩ Grilled ⟨

You can find fresh pineapple rings in most produce departments. Look for the sesame ginger marinade in the barbecue sauce section of your grocery store.

I **pork tenderloin**	**Prepared sesame ginger**
Fresh pineapple rings	**marinade**
I **medium red onion**	**Nonstick cooking spray**

❖ Heat the grill to medium, about 350 degrees.

❖ Trim the silver skin and excess fat from the tenderloins and discard. Cut the tenderloins into 1½-inch chunks.

❖ Cut the pineapple and the red onion into chunks. Thread the tenderloin, pineapple and red onion on metal skewers or bamboo skewers that have been soaked in water for 30 minutes, repeating until all the ingredients are speared. Brush the kabobs liberally with the marinade.

❖ Spray the grill grate with nonstick cooking spray. Grill the kabobs on all sides with the grill cover down for about 12 to 15 minutes, turning the kabobs every 5 minutes.

❖ Remove the skewers and let the kabobs rest on a clean platter under foil for 10 minutes.

❖ Serves 4.

Hot Tips

Grilling is the art of cooking at high heat, and that's what this book is about. Smoking is the art of cooking meats low and slow. Southern barbecue is smoked over hardwood charcoal with other wood for flavoring for many hours to produce the succulent meat so famous in my part of the country.

Pork Fried Rice

This is a great recipe for using up leftover grilled pork chops or grilled tenderloin. It would also work well with grilled shrimp. If your children don't like bean sprouts or snow peas, use vegetables they do like. You don't need a wok for this recipe—any large sauté pan will do.

    2 tablespoons vegetable oil
    8 ounces white mushrooms, sliced
    5 green onions, thinly sliced
 1/2 cup bean sprouts
 1/2 cup snow peas
 1/4 cup diced carrot
    1 teaspoon minced gingerroot
    2 tablespoons soy sauce
    2 teaspoons dark sesame oil
    3 cups cooked rice
    1 cup leftover grilled pork, thinly sliced

❖ Heat the vegetable oil in a large heavy skillet over medium-high heat on the stove. Cook the mushrooms in the hot oil until they are brown and their juice has evaporated. Add the green onions, bean sprouts, snow peas and carrot; sauté the vegetables for about 5 minutes or until tender. Stir in the gingerroot, soy sauce, sesame oil, rice and pork. Mix well and heat through.

❖ Serves 4.

Spicy Sausage with Pasta ❯ **Grilled** ❮

Combining tomato sauce with cream makes a rich sauce.

4 mild Italian sausages
Nonstick cooking spray
I pound penne pasta
2 cups Easy Tomato Sauce (see page 41)
I cup heavy cream
2 tablespoons extra-virgin olive oil
I small onion, thinly sliced
I small yellow bell pepper, cored, cut into strips
I small red bell pepper, cored, cut into strips

❖ Heat the grill to medium, about 350 degrees.

❖ Spray the grill grate with nonstick cooking spray. Grill the sausages with the lid closed until nicely browned on all sides. Remove from the grill and set aside.

❖ Cook the pasta on the stove following the package directions; drain and set aside.

❖ Heat the tomato sauce in a saucepan over medium-low heat on the stove. Stir in the cream and set aside.

❖ Heat the olive oil in a sauté pan over medium-high heat on the stove. Sauté the onion and bell peppers in the hot oil for 5 minutes or until tender and beginning to brown; remove from heat. Cut the sausages into slices and stir them into the onion mixture.

❖ Place the pasta, the tomato mixture and the sausage mixture in a large bowl and toss to combine.

❖ Serves 4 generously.

Italian Sausage Kabobs **Grilled**

Sausage is very forgiving on the grill because of its high fat content. This recipe is good for any kind of sausage, but the spiciness of Italian sausage is a great complement to the sweetness of the pineapple.

6 links mild Italian sausage
1 container fresh pineapple rings or chunks
1 large green bell pepper, cored, seeded, cut into chunks
1 medium yellow onion, cut into chunks
Your favorite barbecue seasoning
Nonstick cooking spray

❖ Heat the grill to medium, about 350 degrees.

❖ Cut the sausages into 1½-inch slices. If the pineapple is in rings, cut it into 1-inch chunks.

❖ Assemble the kabobs by spearing 1 piece of sausage, a chunk of green pepper, a chunk of onion and a pineapple chunk on metal skewers or bamboo skewers that have been soaked in water for 30 minutes. Continue until the skewers are full. Sprinkle liberally with barbecue seasoning.

❖ Spray the grill grate with nonstick cooking spray. Grill the kabobs with the lid open for 12 to 15 minutes, turning every 5 minutes until the sausage is nicely browned. Remove from the grill and serve.

❖ Serves 4.

Chicago-Style Grilled Hot Dogs ❯**Grilled**❮

Grilling hot dogs is the simplest thing in the world because they're already cooked. What you're really doing is browning them. This combination of condiments is famous in Chicago. It can be addictive! The natural casing gives the dogs a nice snap when you bite into them.

> **4 to 6 all-beef hot dogs with natural casings**
> **Butter, softened**
> **4 to 6 hot dog buns**
> **Chopped onion**
> **Pickle relish**
> **Prepared yellow mustard**
> **Dill pickle spears**
> **Tomato slices**
> **Celery seed**

❖ Heat the grill to medium-high, about 400 degrees.

❖ Grill the hot dogs with the lid open for about 3 minutes on each side or until nicely browned, turning once.

❖ Butter the hot dog buns and grill them until golden brown.

❖ To assemble a Chicago Dog, place a hot dog in a bun and top with onion, pickle relish, mustard, a dill pickle spear (cut it in half lengthwise if it's too thick), several tomato slices and a sprinkling of celery seed.

❖ Serves 4 to 6.

Chicken Wings **Grilled**

The beauty of chicken wings is that they are easy to grill and come out perfect almost one-hundred percent of the time. Rubbing the skin with cornstarch makes it unbelievably crispy but it doesn't leave any aftertaste. Trust me—you'll love the difference.

> **8 chicken wings**
> **Mayhew's Special Seasoning (see page 32)**
> **Cornstarch**
> **Nonstick cooking spray**

❖ Heat the grill to medium, about 350 degrees.

❖ Remove the tips of the chicken wings with a sharp knife and discard. Dust the wings with the cornstarch and sprinkle with the Special Seasoning.

❖ Spray the grill grate with nonstick cooking spray. Grill the wings with the lid open for about 20 minutes, turning occasionally so the skin will brown evenly.

❖ Serves 4 as an appetizer or 2 as an entrée.

Hot Tips

Cut up leftover grilled chicken in small thin pieces, and use it the next morning for a school-day breakfast in a chicken quesadilla with grated Cheddar cheese. Just sprinkle grated cheese on a tortilla, top with sliced chicken, and microwave for 30 seconds. Fold, cut, and serve.

Marinated Chicken Kabobs

Chicken, especially breast meat, can dry out quickly on the grill, so I use a marinade to keep it moist. You can concoct your own marinades or use the ones in this book, but sometimes it's easiest just to use a bottled marinade, as in this recipe.

½ cup bottled sesame ginger marinade
3 large chicken breasts, cut into 1½-inch pieces
8 ounces fresh button mushrooms, stems removed
1 green pepper, cored, seeded, cut into chunks
1 medium red onion, cut into chunks

❖ Combine the marinade and the chicken in a heavy-duty gallon plastic bag; seal and place in a bowl or container to guard against leaks. Marinate in the refrigerator for about 4 hours.

❖ Heat the grill to medium, about 350 degrees.

❖ Remove the chicken from the marinade. Spear the chicken pieces, mushrooms, green pepper chunks and onion chunks alternately on metal skewers or on bamboo ones that have been soaked in water for 30 minutes.

❖ Grill the skewers with the lid closed for about 5 minutes per side or until the chicken feels firm when pressed.

❖ Note: If you have leftover mushrooms, peppers and onions, chop them up and sauté them in a little olive oil. They're great added to scrambled eggs in the morning.

❖ Serves 4.

Asian Chicken Salad ▶ Grilled ◀

This is a ridiculously simple but delicious salad. It was inspired by my favorite entrée at a "ladies who lunch" restaurant that closed. I was so desperate for the recipe I experimented until I found the right taste. If you want to jazz it up, you can add sliced green onions, pea pods, and other vegetables, but I love it just as it is.

1 or 2 boneless skinless chicken breasts
Cavender's All Purpose Greek Seasoning®
Nonstick cooking spray
4 packages ramen noodle soup,
seasoning packets discarded
2 tablespoons dark sesame oil
1/2 cup mayonnaise

❖ Heat the grill to medium, about 350 degrees.

❖ Sprinkle the Cavendar's® liberally over both sides of the chicken.

❖ Spray the grill grate with nonstick cooking spray. Place the chicken breasts on the grate and grill with the lid open for about 5 minutes. Turn over the chicken and grill until the internal temperature reaches 165 degrees.

❖ Remove the chicken to a platter and let it stand, covered with foil, for 10 minutes.

❖ Prepare the ramen noodles on the stove using the package directions. Drain the noodles and toss with the sesame oil in a bowl. Let stand until room temperature. Place the noodles and mayonnaise in a medium bowl and stir to combine.

❖ Cut the chicken into thin slices. Place the chicken and noodles mixture in a bowl and toss to combine. Chill, covered, for at least 1 hour before serving.

❖ Serves 4.

Chicken Salad with Dried Cherries

I always grill a few extra chicken breasts so I will have leftovers to make a chicken salad. This is my favorite version.

> **2 grilled boneless skinless chicken breasts**
> **1/3 cup slivered almonds**
> **1/2 cup diced celery**
> **1/2 cup chopped dried cherries**
> **1 cup mayonnaise**
> **Salt and pepper to taste**

❖ Cut the chicken breasts into 1-inch pieces and place in a food processor container. Process until the chicken is the desired consistency for chicken salad.

❖ Heat the oven to 400 degrees. Place the almonds in an ovenproof dish and toast in the oven, shaking occasionally to turn them, for about 10 minutes or until they begin to brown. They will go from brown to scorched in seconds, so watch them carefully.

❖ Place the chicken, almonds, celery, cherries and mayonnaise in a medium bowl; stir gently to combine. Season with salt and pepper. Chill, covered, for 1 hour before serving.

❖ Serves 4.

Sesame Chicken Lettuce Wraps

Here's a delicious way to use up leftover grilled chicken.

> 1 teaspoon dark sesame oil
> 1 tablespoon vegetable oil
> 1½ teaspoons minced garlic
> 1 tablespoon minced gingerroot
> ½ cup sliced scallions
> ½ cup chopped water chestnuts
> 2 cups chopped grilled boneless skinless
>   chicken breasts
> ¼ cup orange juice
> 1 tablespoon soy sauce
> 4 tablespoons hoisin sauce
> 8 to 10 large green leaves of iceberg lettuce
> ⅓ cup crushed peanuts

❖ Heat the sesame oil and the vegetable oil in a large sauté pan over medium heat on the stove. Add the garlic and gingerroot; sauté for 1 minute. Add the scallions and water chestnuts; sauté for 3 to 4 minutes or until the scallions are tender. Remove from heat. Add the chicken, orange juice, soy sauce and hoisin sauce; mix well.

❖ To serve, mound ¼ cup of the chicken mixture in each lettuce leaf and sprinkle with a spoonful of peanuts. Fold the lettuce like a burrito and enjoy!

❖ Serves 4.

Chicken and Stuffing Casserole

Food snobs turn up their noses at recipes with cream of mushroom soup, but you know it's a mom's best friend when it comes to tasty casseroles prepared in a hurry. The smoked paprika really gives this casserole a boost, but if you can't find it, substitute regular paprika.

3 grilled boneless skinless chicken breasts
1 can cream of mushroom soup
1 cup sour cream
½ cup whole milk
1 teaspoon smoked paprika
½ teaspoon salt
1 cup frozen peas
2 (6-ounce) packages stuffing mix

❖ Heat the oven to 350 degrees.
❖ Cut the chicken into bite-sized pieces. Combine the cream of mushroom soup, sour cream, milk, paprika and salt in a large bowl and mix well. Mix in the chicken and peas.
❖ Prepare the stuffing mix using the package directions.
❖ Layer the chicken mixture in a 9x13-inch baking dish. Spread the stuffing mix evenly over the top.
❖ Bake for 30 minutes. If the stuffing has browned too much after 25 minutes, cover it with foil.
❖ Serves 6 to 8.

Currant-Glazed Cornish Game Hens

This recipe uses a method called spatchcocking, which means removing the backbone so the bird will lie flat on the grill. You can substitute peach or apricot jam and Dijon mustard for the currant jelly and stone ground mustard.

4 Cornish game hens
  Mayhew's Special Seasoning
    (see page 32)
  Cornstarch
4 tablespoons red currant jelly

4 teaspoons stone ground
  mustard
2 teaspoons Worcestershire sauce
  Nonstick cooking spray

❖ Heat the grill to medium, about 350 degrees.

❖ Remove the giblets from the game hens, discarding or reserving them for another use. Rinse the hens and pat dry.

❖ Spatchcock the hens by using kitchen shears to cut through both sides of the length of the backbone to remove it (the backbone feels bony; the breast bone is just thin cartilage). Discard the backbone or save it to make chicken stock.

❖ Lay the hens out flat on your work surface. Fold under the wings. Sprinkle the hens liberally with the Special Seasoning and cornstarch.

❖ Heat the currant jelly, mustard and Worcestershire sauce in a small saucepan over low heat on the stove, stirring until blended and smooth. Remove from heat.

❖ Spray the grill grate with nonstick cooking spray. Place the hens on the grill, skin side down. Close the lid and grill for about 9 minutes. Turn over the game hens and brush them with the currant glaze. Insert a probe thermometer in the thickest part of the breast without touching a bone and close the lid. Grill the game hens until the internal temperature reaches 165 degrees.

❖ Remove the game hens to a clean platter and let them stand, covered with foil, for 10 minutes.

❖ Serves 4.

Turkey Hot Browns

If you don't want to grill the bread for this recipe, you can always pop it in the toaster.

8 slices bacon

8 ounces white mushrooms, sliced

Salt and pepper to taste

¼ cup (½ stick) butter

4 tablespoons flour

2 cups whole milk

1 cup shredded sharp white Cheddar cheese

4 slices rustic bread

Grilled turkey breast, sliced

1 large tomato, sliced

❖ Heat the oven to 400 degrees. Arrange the bacon slices in a single layer in a shallow foil-lined baking pan. Bake for 20 minutes. Remove the bacon to paper towels to drain, leaving the drippings in the pan. Crumble the bacon and set aside.

❖ Pour the bacon drippings into a heavy-duty sauté pan over medium-low heat on the stove. Sauté the mushrooms in the hot drippings until they have released their juices and are nicely browned. Season with salt and pepper and set aside.

❖ Melt the butter in a 2-quart saucepan over medium heat on the stove. Add the flour and cook for 1 minute to eliminate the raw taste, whisking constantly. Add the milk slowly and cook for about 10 minutes or until thickened, stirring constantly. Add the cheese and cook until melted, stirring until the mixture is smooth.

❖ Heat the grill to medium-high, about 400 degrees.

❖ Grill the bread until it is lightly charred on both sides.

❖ To assemble the hot browns, place each slice of bread on a plate. Top with turkey slices and tomato slices. Drizzle cheese sauce over the tomatoes and sprinkle with bacon crumbs.

❖ Serves 4.

Creamed Turkey in Puff Pastry Shells

You can find puff pastry in the freezer section of your supermarket. The creamed turkey would be equally good over toasted English muffins. If you don't have Madeira on hand, you can leave it out. It just adds a little extra dimension to the dish.

2 tablespoons butter
8 ounces white mushrooms, sliced
Salt and pepper to taste
1 tablespoon Madeira
1 teaspoon dried thyme
¼ cup (½ stick) butter

¼ cup all-purpose flour
2 cups whole milk
½ cup grated Parmesan cheese
½ teaspoon salt
⅓ cup frozen peas
1½ cups chopped grilled turkey
Puff pastry shells

❖ Melt the 2 tablespoons butter in a heavy sauté pan over medium-high heat on the stove. Add the mushrooms and season to taste with salt and pepper. Sauté the mushrooms until they have released their juices and are nicely browned. Stir in the Madeira and continue cooking until most of the liquid has evaporated. Remove from heat and set aside.

❖ Melt the ¼ cup butter in a 2-quart saucepan over medium heat on the stove. Add the flour and cook for 1 minute to eliminate the raw taste, whisking constantly. Whisk in the milk slowly. Cook for about 10 minutes or until the mixture coats the back of a spoon, stirring constantly; if the sauce gets too thick, add a little more milk. Stir in the Parmesan cheese and the ½ teaspoon salt. Add the mushroom mixture, peas and turkey to the white sauce and mix well.

❖ Bake the puff pastry shells using the package directions.

❖ When the puff pastry shells are done, remove the center portion of each shell and fill with the turkey mixture. Replace the shell cap.

❖ Serves 4.

Smoked Ribs

Unlike grilling, smoking is the art of cooking meats low and slow. While I don't expect a busy mom to sit around for 12 hours tending a fire to produce barbecue, I'll bet a month's worth of new shoes that some of you gals are willing to take 4 hours out of a Saturday to make the best ribs you'll ever eat. So I'm offering one low and slow recipe to introduce you to the art of smoking.

The technique I'm going to teach you for doing ribs is one that's similar to many competition cooks on the circuit. It involves the 2-1-1 method, which means you smoke your ribs for 2 hours on the grill, take them off, wrap them in heavy-duty aluminum foil, put them back on the grill for 1 hour, then unwrap them again, and cook them until they're done, anywhere from 30 minutes to 1 hour. Wrapping the ribs in foil steams them, allowing them to get tender.

I'm not going to lie to you here. The best way to cook these ribs is on a charcoal grill, so that's the way I'm going to do them in this recipe. You can adapt the recipe to a gas grill with a drawer for smoking chips.

There are almost countless rubs (the combination of spices) that can be used for ribs. But for a general recipe, I'm going to recommend a rub that I know everyone can find across the country: Emeril's Original Essence®. It's a good all-purpose rub. Rather than use chunks of wood or wood chips to achieve the smoked flavor, I recommend BBQrs Delight® Wood Pellets (www.bbqrsdelight.com), which are made from real wood. You can find them at most grill stores. Just enclose 1/3 cup of pellets in heavy-duty aluminum foil, poke a tiny hole in the packet with a wooden toothpick and place the packet on the top of the hot coals. By the way, BBQrs Delight is also owned by a woman, Candy Weaver, who's much better at competition barbecue than the team I'm on, Chicks in Charge, but we still like her anyway.

2 racks of baby back ribs	*Equipment you will need:*
Extra-virgin olive oil	**Aluminum half-pans**
Emeril's Original Essence®	**Heavy-duty aluminum foil**
Squeeze butter	**Charcoal briquettes (I recommend**
Honey	**Kingsford® Charcoal)**
	BBQrs Delight® Wood Pellets,
	hickory or oak flavor

❖ Bank about 30 briquettes on one side of your grill. Place an aluminum half-pan on the other side to catch the fat from the ribs. Light the charcoal; keep the grill vents open and the lid up until the coals are ashed over. Then put the metal end of a probe thermometer on the grate, close the lid and close the vents on the drip pan side. You want the temperature to be between 220 degrees and 250 degrees. It will take about 30 minutes.

❖ While the grill is heating, remove the membrane from the back of each rib by inserting an index finger underneath the membrane and pulling it off (sometimes a paper towel helps to get a good grip).

❖ Rub the ribs with olive oil and liberally apply the Emeril's Original Essence. When the grill temperature is between 220 degrees and 250 degrees, remove the grill grate and place a foil packet of BBQrs Delight pellets on the coals; replace the grate. Add the ribs on one side of the grate and another aluminum half-pan of water on the other (if the half-pan won't fit, use a smaller heat-proof container) to help keep the ribs moist. Keep the probe on the grate so you can monitor the temperature. Close the lid. Make sure the vent on the charcoal side is wide open and the vent on the drip pan side of the grill is closed. If there are any vents on the top of the grill, they should also be open.

❖ Smoke for 2 hours, checking occasionally to see that the temperature is stable. If it starts to dip you will have to add more charcoal. Don't panic; just remove the grate with the ribs and water pan still on it, add briquettes and replace the grate.

❖ After 2 hours, remove each rack of ribs to a sheet of heavy-duty aluminum foil. Apply a liberal amount of squeeze butter and honey, rubbing them evenly into the ribs. Fold up the foil to enclose the ribs, sealing both ends to guard against leakage.

❖ Place the foil-enclosed ribs on the grill and cook for 1 hour. Remove the ribs from the foil and return them to the grill for at least 30 minutes longer. To test for doneness, cut off an end and taste it, or pick up a rack in the middle—if both sides droop, it is done.

❖ If you like your ribs with sauce, brush it on 10 minutes before you remove the ribs from the grill. Remove the ribs to a platter and let them stand, wrapped in foil, for at least 15 minutes.

❖ Serves 4 to 6.

Seafood

Chapter Eight

Fish and kids sometimes don't go together.

My good friend, JoAnn Grose, and I used to take her two daughters to a seafood restaurant in Charlotte, N.C. She would tell the girls she was going to order them fish sticks. One night, I took a close look at the menu and said—apparently too loudly—that they didn't offer fish sticks. She gave me a dagger look and muttered that she cut a fried fish filet into strips so the girls would eat them.

Grilled fish can become your child's favorite if you select the right variety. And the charm of grilled fish is that it just takes minutes to prepare.

Some Seafood Tips

The best kinds of fish to select for children are mild fish such as tilapia, flounder, mahi-mahi, orange roughy, or catfish. Fattier fish such as salmon or tuna don't seem to go over as well.

The biggest trick to grilling fish is to make sure it doesn't stick to the grill. I always use an oiled grill basket, and I also always oil both sides of the fish, either with extra-virgin olive oil or with nonstick cooking spray.

It doesn't take long to grill fish. After you've grilled the fish on one side and flipped it, test it with a fork after about 2 minutes. If it's beginning to flake, it's done.

Shellfish such as shrimp are great on the grill. Shrimp have their own built-in thermometers. When they turn pink, they're ready to eat.

Crab legs are also great on the grill, but remember they're already cooked. All you need to do is heat them through. The advantage to doing that versus boiling them is that you don't have a big mess in the kitchen, and you also avoid that "crabby" smell permeating the house.

Bayou Catfish **Grilled**

Catfish is extremely moist, making it very good for the grill.

4 catfish filets, about ½-inch thick
Nonstick cooking spray

Cajun seasoning (such as Papa Tony's®
New Orleans Shrimp Mix)

❖ Heat the grill to medium-high, about 400 degrees.
❖ Rinse the catfish filets under cold water and pat dry. Spray with nonstick cooking spray and apply the Cajun seasoning liberally.
❖ Place the fish in a grill basket that has been sprayed with nonstick cooking spray. Grill with the lid closed for 3 minutes. Turn over the catfish and grill for 2 minutes longer or until the fish flakes slightly when tested with a fork.
❖ Serve with Cajun Tartar Sauce (see page 35) and lemon wedges.
❖ Serves 4.

Garlic Butter-Basted Tilapia

Garlic butter makes just about anything better, especially grilled fish. Tilapia is so mild that most children like it, even if they turn up their noses at other seafood.

¹/₂ cup (1 stick) butter
2 garlic cloves, peeled, sliced
4 tilapia filets
   Cajun seasoning
   Salt and pepper to taste

❖ Melt the butter in a small saucepan over low heat on the stove; add the garlic. Heat gently for about 15 minutes until the garlic infuses the butter. Remove from heat and cool slightly. Remove the garlic with a slotted spoon.

❖ Heat the grill to medium, about 350 degrees.

❖ Brush both sides of the tilapia with the melted butter mixture and place the filets in a grill basket. Sprinkle both sides of the filets with Cajun seasoning, and season with salt and pepper.

❖ Grill the filets with the lid closed for about 4 minutes. Turn over the filets and grill for about 2 minutes or until the fish flakes slightly when tested with a fork.

❖ Serves 4.

Grilled Fish Tacos

These grilled fish tacos are a lot healthier than the fried version.

2 grilled tilapia filets
1/2 cup mayonnaise
1/4 cup sour cream
1 teaspoon fresh lemon juice
1 tablespoon fresh dill
Salt and pepper to taste
Vegetable oil
8 corn tortillas
3 cups shredded cabbage

❖ Heat the filets for 15 seconds in the microwave or until warm.

❖ Break the tilapia filets into pieces.

❖ Combine the mayonnaise, sour cream, lemon juice and dill in a medium bowl; mix well. Season with salt and pepper.

❖ Heat a thin layer of vegetable oil in a skillet over medium heat on the stove. Fry the tortillas on both sides until they are heated through and pliable. Drain on paper towels.

❖ Stack 2 corn tortillas together to make each taco. Fill each taco with 1/4 of the tilapia, 1/4 of the cabbage and 1/4 of the mayonnaise mixture. Fold the tacos over and serve.

❖ Serves 4.

Balsamic Honey-Glazed Salmon

The balance of sweet and sour from the honey and vinegar cuts through the richness of the grilled salmon.

½ cup balsamic vinegar	**Salt and pepper to taste**
2 tablespoons honey	**Nonstick cooking spray**
1 (16-ounce) piece of skinless salmon	

❖ Heat the grill to medium, about 350 degrees.

❖ Combine the balsamic vinegar and honey in a small saucepan over medium-high heat on the stove. Cook until the mixture is reduced by half, stirring occasionally.

❖ Brush the salmon liberally with the balsamic honey glaze. Season with salt and pepper.

❖ Spray a grill basket or pan with nonstick cooking spray and place the salmon in it. Grill with the lid closed for about 5 minutes. Turn over the salmon and grill for 5 minutes longer or until the fish flakes easily when tested with a fork but is still moist. Remove the salmon to a platter and brush additional balsamic honey glaze over the top. Let it stand, covered with foil, for 10 minutes before serving.

❖ Serves 4.

Hot Tips

Leftover grilled salmon is good cold with
a sour cream dill sauce.

Salmon Salad | Leftover |

If you like tuna salad, you'll love salmon salad. Just make this tasty recipe from leftover grilled salmon. It's great for sandwiches or served on crackers for an appetizer.

5 ounces grilled salmon	**½ cup mayonnaise**
¼ cup diced celery	**1 tablespoon sour cream**
1 tablespoon minced shallot	**Salt and pepper to taste**
1 teaspoon dried dill	

❖ Cut the salmon into chunks. Combine the salmon, celery, shallot, dill, mayonnaise and sour cream in a small bowl; mix with a fork to break up the salmon. Season with salt and pepper.

❖ Yields about 2 cups.

Salmon Spread | Leftover |

This is as easy to put together as it is delicious.

1 cup leftover Balsamic Honey-Glazed Salmon (see page 109)	**1 tablespoon thinly sliced green onion**
8 ounces cream cheese, softened	**1 teaspoon Mayhew's Special Seasoning (see page 32)**
1 teaspoon Worcestershire sauce	

❖ Cut the salmon into small pieces. Combine the salmon, cream cheese, Worcestershire sauce, green onion and Special Seasoning in a medium bowl; mix well with a fork. Serve with crackers or on bread.

❖ Yields about 2 cups.

Ginger Lime-Marinated Tuna ❯ **Grilled** ❯

There are two schools of thought on grilling tuna. Some like it cooked all the way through, while others just quickly sear it so the outside is charred but the inside is still raw. I kind of split the difference because I find thoroughly cooked tuna too dry. I grill it until it's almost cooked through but still pink in the center.

Ponzu is kind of a kicked-up soy sauce made with lemon juice and other flavorings. You can find it next to the soy sauce in your grocery store.

1/2 **cup extra-virgin olive oil**
3 **tablespoons fresh lime juice**
1 **teaspoon minced fresh gingerroot**
2 **tablespoons roughly chopped cilantro**
2 **tablespoons ponzu**
4 **(5-ounce) fresh yellowfin tuna steaks,**
about 1 inch thick
Salt and pepper to taste
Nonstick cooking spray

❖ Combine the olive oil, lime juice, gingerroot, cilantro and ponzu in a small bowl; mix well. Place the tuna steaks in a shallow dish. Add the ponzu mixture, being sure to coat the tuna evenly. Marinate, covered with plastic wrap, in the refrigerator for 30 minutes, turning the steaks once.

❖ Heat the grill to medium, about 350 degrees.

❖ Remove the steaks from the marinade and brush off the cilantro and the gingerroot.

❖ Spray the grill pan with nonstick cooking spray and place the tuna steaks in the pan. Grill with the lid closed for 4 minutes. Turn over the tuna and grill for 4 minutes longer. Remove the tuna steaks to a platter and let them stand, covered with foil, for 10 minutes before serving.

❖ Serves 4.

The Best Tuna Salad

While you're making the Ginger Lime Marinated Tuna on page 111, throw an extra tuna steak on the grill for this kicked-up tuna salad. You should be able to find currants in your local health foods grocery store, but if you don't, substitute raisins.

1 (5-ounce) tuna steak, grilled
¼ cup chopped celery
1 tablespoon chopped red onion
1 tablespoon currants or raisins
1 tablespoon sunflower seeds
½ cup mayonnaise
¼ teaspoon curry powder
Salt and pepper to taste

❖ Cut the tuna steak into chunks. Combine the tuna, celery, red onion, currants, sunflower seeds, mayonnaise, curry powder, salt and pepper in a medium bowl. Mix well, using a fork to break up the tuna chunks.

❖ Yields about 2 cups.

Hot Tips

Line everything you can with heavy-duty aluminum foil—baking pans, cookie sheets, anything that will hold foil. It makes clean-up a breeze.

Shrimp with Garlic Citrus Butter ▶ Grilled

The biggest trick to grilling shrimp is to not overcook them. Shrimp have their own natural thermometer—when they turn pink they're done.

¹/₂ cup (1 stick) butter
1 teaspoon minced garlic
¹/₄ teaspoon chili powder
¹/₄ teaspoon pepper
2 tablespoons fresh lemon juice
1 pound fresh shrimp (10 to 15 count*)

❖ Heat the grill to medium, about 350 degrees.

❖ Melt the butter in a saucepan over low heat on the stove. Stir in the garlic, chili powder, pepper and lemon juice.

❖ Remove the shells from the shrimp. Run the tip of a sharp knife down the back of each shrimp and remove the vein. Spear the shrimp on metal skewers or on bamboo ones that have been soaked in water for 30 minutes. Brush each shrimp with the butter mixture (there will be some left over for dipping).

❖ Place the shrimp skewers on the grill and grill with the lid open for 3 minutes. Turn over the skewers and grill for 3 minutes longer or until the shrimp turn pink.

❖ Serves 4.

*10 to 15 count means there are 10 to 15 head-off shrimp in a pound. These larger shrimp are easy to put on a skewer.

Shrimp Cocktail ⟩ **Grilled** ⟨

This recipe doesn't use a conventional ketchup-based cocktail sauce, but if that's what you would like to use, it will work well, too.

6 tablespoons extra-virgin olive oil
1 tablespoon paprika
Pinch of black pepper
¼ teaspoon salt
1 tablespoon minced onion
4 tablespoons prepared yellow mustard
2 tablespoons red wine vinegar
1 pound fresh shrimp (10 to 15 count*)
Nonstick cooking spray

❖ Combine the olive oil, paprika, pepper, salt, onion and mustard in a small bowl and whisk to blend. Whisk in the vinegar. Chill, covered, for at least 30 minutes before serving.

❖ Heat the grill to medium, about 350 degrees.

❖ Remove the shells from the shrimp. Run the tip of a sharp knife down the back of each shrimp and remove the vein. Spear the shrimp on metal skewers or on bamboo ones that have been soaked in water for 30 minutes. Spray both sides of the shrimp lightly with nonstick cooking spray.

❖ Place the skewered shrimp on the grill and grill with the lid open for 3 minutes. Turn over the skewers and grill for 3 minutes longer or until the shrimp turn pink. Serve with the mustard sauce.

❖ Serves 4.

*10 to 15 count means there are 10 to 15 head-off shrimp in a pound. These larger shrimp are easy to put on a skewer.

Creamy Shrimp Enchiladas

When you're grilling shrimp, throw on an extra pound just so you can make this simple and scrumptious casserole. This enchilada casserole also freezes well.

1 pound grilled shrimp, tails removed
1 tablespoon vegetable oil
1/2 cup chopped orange or yellow bell pepper
1 small onion, chopped
1 teaspoon grill seasoning (such as McCormick®
   Grill Mates® Montreal Steak Seasoning)
8 ounces cream cheese, softened
5 (8-inch) flour tortillas
   Nonstick cooking spray
1 1/2 cups shredded mozzarella cheese
1 cup heavy cream

❖ Heat the oven to 350 degrees.

❖ Cut the grilled shrimp into bite-sized pieces.

❖ Heat the vegetable oil in a sauté pan over medium-high heat on the stove. Add the bell pepper, onion and grill seasoning. Sauté over medium heat for 5 to 10 minutes or until the onion is translucent and the bell pepper is tender.

❖ Reduce the heat to low. Add the cream cheese and heat until melted, stirring constantly. Remove from heat. Stir in the shrimp.

❖ Scoop equal portions of the shrimp mixture into the tortillas. Roll each tortilla into a cylinder. Arrange the rolled tortillas seam side down in a 9x9-inch glass baking dish that has been sprayed lightly with nonstick cooking spray.

❖ Sprinkle the shredded mozzarella cheese over the tortillas and drizzle with the cream.

❖ Bake for 30 to 45 minutes or until light brown and bubbly.

❖ Serves 5.

Shrimp Salad Leftover

A scoop of this shrimp salad is excellent over shredded iceberg lettuce.

2 cups leftover grilled shrimp, coarsely chopped
1/2 cup mayonnaise
2 tablespoons ketchup
1 teaspoon fresh lemon juice
1 tablespoon pickle relish
1/4 cup chopped celery
Salt and pepper to taste

❖ Combine the shrimp, mayonnaise, ketchup, lemon juice, pickle relish and celery in a bowl and mix well. Season with salt and pepper. Chill until serving time.

❖ Yields about 2 cups.

Hot Tips

If you're an ebay shopper, type in the word bbq and look at all the great equipment and wacky accessories available.

Alaskan King Crab Legs ▶ **Grilled** ◀

This is more of a procedure than a recipe. Crab legs always come precooked, so the trick is to heat them without making the delicate meat tough. Many recipes call for boiling the crab legs, but then you run the risk of waterlogging the meat. Putting them on the grill is a simple and no-mess way to get them hot.

> **1 pound Alaskan king crab legs**
> **1/2 cup (1 stick) butter**

❖ Heat the grill to medium, about 350 degrees.

❖ Arrange the crab legs on the grate. Grill with the lid closed for about 7 minutes, just until the crab legs are heated through.

❖ Melt the butter in a small saucepan either on the grill or over medium heat on the stove. Remove the tough outer shell of the crab legs by cutting through it with a pair of kitchen scissors. Serve the crab meat with the melted butter for dipping.

❖ Serves 4 as an appetizer or 2 as a main course.

Pizzas

Most people don't think of the grill when it comes to pizza, but your grill—gas or charcoal—is the way to make the best pizza you will ever eat. You can heat your grill to 500 degrees and achieve that same crisp crust that wood-fired pizza ovens produce.

You can also make the crust as thick or thin as you like and expand on the toppings that are usually available at a pizza shop. Making your own pizzas is also a great way to use up leftovers in the refrigerator. Have some leftover grilled vegetables and chicken? Add some tomato sauce or pesto, a bit of grated cheese and you're good to go.

Ingredients and Equipment

You'll need a few ingredients and pieces of equipment to get started. You'll need pizza dough, of course. Some grocery stores carry pizza dough in their bakery departments, or you can go to a local pizzeria and buy just the dough balls. You'll need a little flour for the work surface so the dough doesn't stick.

You'll need a rolling pin to roll out the dough. (I'd love to think you could throw the dough in the air and it would come back in a perfectly shaped circle, but let's get real here.) To slip the pizza onto the grill, you'll want a pizza peel (a giant wooden paddle) or at the least, a large cutting board. You'll also need a pizza stone as a cooking surface for your pie. Pizza stones are available at most houseware stores, and they're worth the cost because using them is the only way to ensure a crispy crust.

The trick to getting a good crispy pizza crust is to heat up the pizza stone well in advance, at least 15 minutes and half an hour is better. To get an easy slide onto the stone, sprinkle cornmeal (the coarse kind, not cornmeal flour or mix) on the pizza peel before you put the dough on. Then sprinkle a little more cornmeal on the heated stone, and your pizza will slide on and off with ease.

Each ball of dough available from the supermarket makes two pizzas that are about 12 inches in diameter if the dough is rolled out thinly. The recipes in this chapter are good for one pizza, and in our family, one of those pizzas is good for three people.

And don't be too concerned about following the ingredient list exactly. Pizzas are like casseroles—there are no hard and fast rules.

Hot Tips

Have a "forage" night once in awhile. When you have multiple leftovers in the refrigerator, announce it's forage night and let the family clean out the refrigerator and spare you a night of cooking.

Onion and Prosciutto Pizza  Grilled

Prosciutto is an Italian ham that is available at most grocery deli counters. It is pricey but good, and this recipe doesn't use much of it.

> 1 tablespoon extra-virgin olive oil
> 1 medium sweet onion (such as Vidalia),
>   sliced in thin rings
> 1 purchased ball of pizza dough
>   Flour
>   Cornmeal
> 1/2 teaspoon dried oregano
> 6 ounces sliced provolone cheese
> 4 thin slices prosciutto

❖ Heat the grill to 500 degrees with the pizza stone on the grill and the lid closed.

❖ Heat a large sauté pan over medium heat on the stove. Pour the olive oil into the hot pan. Sauté the onions in the olive oil for about 20 minutes or until they turn a deep caramel color. If the pan appears dry, add a little more oil.

❖ Divide the pizza dough in half; refrigerate half or use it all and double the recipe. Roll the dough into a circle of the desired thinness on a lightly floured surface. Slide the dough onto a pizza peel that has been dusted with cornmeal. Sprinkle the oregano over the dough. Cover with the slices of provolone cheese and prosciutto. Spread the caramelized onions over the top.

❖ Sprinkle additional cornmeal over the pizza stone. Remove the pizza to the stone. Grill with the lid closed for about 8 minutes or until desired doneness, checking frequently after the first 5 minutes.

❖ Serves 3.

Loaded Sausage Pizza **Grilled**

Half a pound of sausage seems like a lot, but it turns out to be just the right amount. You may substitute ground chuck for the sausage if you like.

> ½ **pound bulk pork sausage**
> ¼ **pound white mushrooms, sliced**
> 1 **purchased ball of pizza dough**
> **Flour**
> **Cornmeal**
> 1 **(14-ounce) jar pizza sauce**
> 1 ½ **cups shredded mozzarella cheese**

❖ Heat the grill to 500 degrees with the pizza stone on the grill and the lid closed.

❖ Brown the sausage in a large sauté pan over medium-high heat on the stove, breaking up the meat into small pieces. (Making sure it really begins to turn brown is the secret to great cooked sausage or ground beef.) Drain on paper towels, leaving about 2 tablespoons of the drippings in the pan.

❖ Sauté the mushrooms in the sausage drippings until browned.

❖ Divide the pizza dough in half; refrigerate half or use it all and double the recipe. Roll the dough into a circle of the desired thinness on a lightly floured surface. Slide the dough onto a pizza peel that has been dusted with cornmeal. Layer the pizza sauce, mushrooms, sausage and mozzarella cheese over the dough.

❖ Sprinkle additional cornmeal over the pizza stone. Remove the pizza to the stone. Grill with the lid closed for about 8 minutes or until desired doneness, checking frequently after the first 5 minutes.

❖ Serves 3.

Cheesesteak Pizza **Grilled**

This is my version of a Philly Cheesesteak.

1	tablespoon vegetable oil
1	small green bell pepper, cored, cut into strips
1	small onion, cut into rings
4 or 5	frozen thin steak slices
9	ounces sliced provolone (about 10 slices)
	Flour
1	purchased ball of pizza dough
	Cornmeal

❖ Heat the grill to 500 degrees with the pizza stone on the grill and the lid closed.

❖ Heat the oil in a heavy sauté pan and cook the bell pepper and onions until they are translucent but still slightly crisp. Remove the vegetables with a slotted spoon and set aside.

❖ Cook the steak slices in the same sauté pan using the package directions (sometimes frozen steak slices come two to a portion, so pay attention to the directions). Set aside.

❖ Roll the dough into a circle of the desired thinness on a lightly floured surface. Slide the dough onto a pizza peel that has been dusted with cornmeal. Layer half the provolone slices, the steak slices and the onion mixture over the dough. Top with the remaining provolone slices.

❖ Sprinkle additional cornmeal over the pizza stone. Remove the pizza to the stone. Grill with the lid closed for about 8 minutes or until desired doneness, checking frequently after the first 5 minutes.

❖ Serves 3.

Chicken Pesto Pizza ▶ Grilled ◀

This is my son Noah's all-time favorite pizza. He loads on the mushrooms, but if your kids don't like mushrooms, pick another vegetable they do like.

1/2 teaspoon extra-virgin olive oil
1/4 pound white mushrooms, sliced
1/2 teaspoon extra-virgin olive oil
1/2 cup sliced red bell pepper
1 purchased ball of pizza dough
Flour
1 (7-ounce) container pesto
1 cup chopped leftover grilled chicken breast
1 1/2 cups shredded mozzarella cheese
Cornmeal

❖ Heat the grill to 500 degrees with the pizza stone on the grill and the lid closed.

❖ Heat 1/2 teaspoon olive oil in a sauté pan over medium-high heat on the stove; sauté the mushrooms until browned. Remove the mushrooms with a slotted spoon. Add another 1/2 teaspoon olive oil to the oil remaining in the pan; sauté the bell pepper strips in the oil until tender. Remove from heat.

❖ Roll the dough into a circle of the desired thinness on a lightly floured surface. Slide the dough onto a pizza peel that has been dusted with cornmeal.

❖ Spread desired amount of pesto over the pizza (you will not use a whole container of pesto unless you just love the stuff). Layer the chicken, mushrooms and bell pepper slices over the pesto layer. Sprinkle the mozzarella cheese evenly over the top.

❖ Sprinkle additional cornmeal over the pizza stone. Remove the pizza to the stone. Grill with the lid closed for about 8 minutes or until desired doneness, checking frequently after the first 5 minutes.

❖ Serves 3.

Mediterranean Pita Pizzas

Pita pizzas are an easy, quick way to fix a snack for your kids. You can make the toppings simple, or a little more exotic (as these pitas are). You can find feta cheese crumbles in most dairy cases at the supermarket.

1 onion, sliced into thin rings
Extra-virgin olive oil
Salt and pepper to taste
4 whole pita breads
Sun-dried tomato spread
¾ cup green or black olives, sliced
1 (6-ounce) container crumbled feta cheese

❖ Heat the grill to medium-low, about 325 degrees.

❖ Heat a large sauté pan over medium heat on the stove. Sauté the onion in the olive oil in the pan for about 20 minutes or until the onions turn a deep caramel color. Season with salt and pepper. If the pan appears dry, add a little more oil. Remove from heat.

❖ Separate each pita bread into 2 rounds using the natural opening in the bread. Brush the bottoms of the pitas with olive oil. Layer sun-dried tomato spread over each round. Layer half the sautéed onions over each round. Sprinkle the olives evenly over the onion layer.

❖ Grill the pita pizzas with the lid open for 2 to 3 minutes or until the bottoms are nicely browned. Remove from the grill and sprinkle with feta cheese.

❖ Serves 4 to 8.

Ground Beef and Mushroom Calzone

A calzone is just a pizza folded over and sealed so the topping becomes a filling. They're fun for kids to eat because they're like giant pizza sandwiches. Learn the technique for making the calzones and then invent your own favorite fillings.

1 tablespoon extra-virgin olive oil	1 cup pizza sauce
12 ounces white mushrooms, sliced	1 purchased ball of pizza dough
1 pound ground chuck	Flour
	Shredded Cheddar cheese
	Cornmeal

❖ Heat the grill to medium-high, about 400 degrees, with the pizza stone on the grill and the lid closed.

❖ Heat the olive oil in a heavy sauté pan over medium-high heat on the stove. Sauté the mushrooms in the hot oil for 5 to 10 minutes or until golden brown. Remove from heat.

❖ Brown the ground chuck in a skillet, stirring until crumbly; drain. Combine the mushrooms, ground chuck and pizza sauce in a large bowl and mix well. If the mixture looks too dry, stir in additional pizza sauce.

❖ Divide the pizza dough into 4 portions. Roll each portion into a ¼-inch-thick circle on a large cutting board dusted with flour.

❖ Spread about a cup of the meat mixture over half of each of the dough circles, to within 1 inch of the edge (there may be meat mixture left over). Sprinkle the filling evenly with desired amount of shredded cheese. Fold over the dough to enclose the filling and seal the edges with olive oil. Press the dough edges with a fork to seal in the filling.

❖ Sprinkle the cornmeal over the pizza stone and slide the calzones onto the stone. Grill with the lid closed for about 3 minutes or until the dough is golden brown, checking after the first 2 minutes.

❖ Serves 4.

Pizza Sticks **Grilled**

These are great snacks for the kids. We enjoy these with Olive Oil Dipping Sauce (see page 37). If your kids don't like olive oil, use a prepared pizza sauce or spaghetti sauce as a dip.

1 purchased ball of pizza dough
Flour
Cornmeal
Extra-virgin olive oil
2 tablespoons Italian seasoning
1 cup grated Parmesan cheese

❖ Heat the grill to 500 degrees with the pizza stone on the grill and the lid closed.

❖ Divide the dough into halves. Roll each half into a square or rectangle of desired thinness on a lightly floured surface.

❖ Remove the dough to a pizza peel that has been dusted with cornmeal. Brush the dough with olive oil and sprinkle half the Italian seasoning and half the Parmesan cheese over each dough rectangle. Dust the pizza stone with cornmeal. Slide the dough rectangles onto the stone.

❖ Grill the pizza sticks with the lid closed for about 6 minutes or until desired doneness, checking after 4 minutes.

❖ Cut into strips and serve.

❖ Yields about 8 strips.

Sandwiches

Chapter Ten

The grill makes great sandwiches. Just think of it as an outdoor griddle.

Throw a great summer party by putting all the sandwich fixings on a large tray and letting the kids create their own masterpieces. Then, of course, the resident expert griller—that would be you—can finish them off.

You can also make your grill into a panini maker by the use of a heavy cast iron skillet. Just put the skillet on the top of the sandwich and press—but make sure you have a good pot holder handy!

Pork Loin Sandwiches with Onions [Leftover]

I've been known to grill pork tenderloin just for sandwiches—serve slices on yeast rolls with horseradish mayonnaise as part of a party buffet.

> 1 **medium onion**
> 1 **tablespoon extra-virgin olive oil**
> 6 to 8 **slices leftover Glazed Pork Tenderloin Filets (see page 87)**
> **Prepared honey mustard**
> 4 **Kaiser rolls, split**
> **Havarti cheese, sliced**

❖ Slice the onion into thin rings. Heat the olive oil in a heavy sauté pan over medium heat on the stove. Cook the onion slowly for about 20 minutes or until wilted and nutty brown, stirring occasionally.

❖ Reheat the pork tenderloin filets in the microwave for about 15 seconds.

❖ To build the sandwiches, spread the honey mustard over the cut sides of the Kaiser rolls. Fill the sandwiches with pork tenderloin, Havarti cheese and onions.

❖ Serves 4.

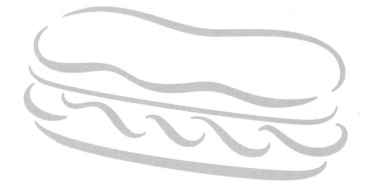

Super Chicken Sausage Sandwiches  Grilled

Chicken sausage comes in a variety of flavors, from sun-dried tomato to Cajun and more. Try several types, and then pick your favorite.

4 flavored chicken sausages
2 tablespoons extra-virgin olive oil
1 red bell pepper, cored, cut into strips
**1 sweet onion (such as a Vidalia), peeled,
    cut into rings**
1/2 cup mayonnaise
**2 tablespoons coarse-grained mustard
    Butter**
4 hoagie rolls, split

❖ Heat the grill to medium, about 350 degrees.

❖ Grill the sausages until they are browned on all sides.

❖ Brush the olive oil over the bell pepper strips and onion rings and place the vegetables in a grill basket. Grill over medium heat until nicely charred.

❖ Combine the mayonnaise and mustard in a small bowl and whisk to blend.

❖ Butter the cut sides of the hoagie rolls. Grill them butter side down until they begin to char.

❖ Assemble the sandwiches by spreading the mayonnaise mixture over the cut sides of the hoagie rolls and filling with the sausages and vegetables.

❖ Serves 4.

Caprese Sandwich ⟩ **Grilled** ⟨

A caprese salad is made of fresh mozzarella, tomato, and basil. This sandwich takes the same ingredients and pumps them up with a pesto mayonnaise. It's important to use fresh mozzarella, which you should find at the gourmet cheese counter in your grocery store.

> **2 teaspoons prepared pesto**
> **1/2 cup mayonnaise**
> **8 slices rustic bread**
> **8 to 10 tomato slices**
> **12 slices fresh mozzarella cheese**
> **Extra-virgin olive oil**

❖ Heat the grill to medium, about 350 degrees.

❖ Whisk the pesto and mayonnaise together in a small bowl. Spread the pesto mixture over one side of each slice of bread. Layer 1/4 of the tomato slices and 1/4 of the mozzarella cheese over the pesto side of each of 4 slices of bread. Top with the remaining bread slices, pesto sides against the mozzarella.

❖ Brush the top of each sandwich with olive oil, and place it oil side down on the grill. Brush the other side of each sandwich with additional olive oil.

❖ Grill with the lid closed for 2 to 3 minutes per side or until toasted, checking frequently to make sure the bread doesn't burn.

❖ Serves 4.

Grilled Bologna Sandwich

Grilled bologna is a signature food of greasy spoon diners, especially in the South. Grilling the bologna makes it almost melt in your mouth. It's definitely not a diet item, but it's worth the calories. The bologna may be grilled in a sauté pan on the stove if you prefer.

4 (¼-inch) slices deli bologna
8 slices bread
4 slices American cheese
   Butter
4 slices tomato
4 lettuce leaves
   Mayonnaise

❖ Heat the grill to medium, about 350 degrees.

❖ Score the bologna edges by making small cuts around the outside of the slices so they won't curl. Place the bologna slices on the grill, and cook them until the edges brown, flipping once. Remove from the grill.

❖ Heat a large sauté pan over medium-high heat on the stove. Butter one side of each slice of bread. Place half the bread slices in the pan, butter side down; top each with grilled bologna and a slice of cheese. Cover with the remaining bread slices, butter side up. Sauté the sandwiches until both sides of the bread are golden, turning once. Remove the sandwiches from the pan and add tomato, lettuce and mayonnaise as desired.

❖ Serves 4.

Pimento Cheese Sandwiches **Grilled**

If you don't want to bother making pimento cheese, the store-bought variety works equally well.

16 ounces sharp Cheddar cheese, shredded
1 (4-ounce) jar chopped pimentos, drained
Mayonnaise
4 to 6 drops hot sauce
8 slices sturdy bread
Butter, softened

❖ Heat the grill to medium, about 350 degrees.

❖ Combine the Cheddar cheese and pimentos in a small bowl. Stir in enough mayonnaise to make of spreading consistency. Add the hot sauce and mix well.

❖ Spread the pimento mixture over 4 slices of bread; top with the remaining 4 bread slices.

❖ Spread butter over 1 side of each sandwich and place on the grill, butter side down. Spread butter over the other sides of the sandwiches.

❖ Grill with the lid closed for 2 to 3 minutes per side or until golden brown, checking frequently to make sure the bread doesn't burn.

❖ Serves 4.

Vegetable and Chicken Wraps · Leftover

This burrito uses leftover grilled vegetables, but you can grill up some peppers, onions, and whatever else you like especially for this sandwich.

8 ounces cream cheese, softened
2 teaspoons dried Italian herbs
4 (10-inch) flour tortillas
2 cups coarsely chopped grilled vegetables
2 grilled chicken breasts, thinly sliced
2 cups baby spinach leaves

❖ Combine the cream cheese and herbs in a bowl; stir to blend.

❖ Spread ¼ of the cream cheese mixture evenly over each tortilla. Layer the grilled vegetables, chicken slices and spinach leaves over the cream cheese mixture. Roll each tortilla into a wrap.

❖ Heat a sauté pan over medium-high heat on the stove. Toast the wraps in the pan for 3 to 5 minutes or until lightly browned on each side. Cut each wrap in half diagonally.

❖ Serves 4.

Hot Tips

Bake bacon in a 400-degree oven on a foil-lined rimmed cookie sheet for 20 minutes, turning after 15 minutes. Drain and refrigerate in a plastic container. Use it crumbled over a salad, in sandwiches, or as part of a bacon biscuit for a quick breakfast. You can also put the cooked bacon in the freezer and use it as the need arises.

Tomato Pesto Chicken Wraps

This sandwich would also be good with leftover turkey. You may substitute basil pesto for the sun-dried tomato pesto.

> **2 grilled chicken breasts**
> **4 (10-inch) flour tortillas**
> **Cream cheese, softened**
>
> **Prepared sun-dried tomato pesto**
> **1 medium red onion, thinly sliced**
> **Green leaf lettuce**

❖ Slice the chicken into thin strips. Spread each tortilla with a thin layer of cream cheese and a thin layer of tomato pesto. Layer the chicken strips, onion slices and lettuce over the pesto layer. Roll each tortilla into a wrap.

❖ Heat a sauté pan over medium-high heat on the stove. Toast the wraps in the pan for 3 to 5 minutes or until lightly browned on each side. Cut each wrap in half diagonally.

❖ Serves 4.

Mexican Chicken Pitas

This recipe can be made in any amount. It just depends on how big a crowd you're feeding.

> **½ cup sour cream**
> **½ cup prepared salsa**
> **2 large pita breads**
>
> **2 grilled chicken breasts, chopped**
> **1 cup shredded pepperjack cheese**
> **1 cup shredded iceberg lettuce**

❖ Combine the sour cream and salsa in a small bowl and mix well.

❖ Separate each pita bread into 2 rounds using the natural opening in the bread. Layer ¼ of the chicken over each round and top with desired amount of the salsa mixture. Sprinkle with shredded pepperjack cheese and lettuce.

❖ Serves 4.

Three-Cheese Flips ◆ Grilled

Flips are just tortillas with a filling, folded in half, and then finished on the grill.

1 generous cup shredded Havarti cheese
1 generous cup shredded Colby cheese
2 tablespoons grated Parmesan cheese
4 tomato slices
 Dash of dried oregano
2 (8-inch) flour tortillas
 Melted butter

❖ Heat the grill to medium-low, about 325 degrees.

❖ Place the Havarti cheese, Colby cheese and Parmesan cheese in a medium bowl and toss to combine. Layer half the cheese mixture over half of each tortilla. Layer 2 of the tomato slices over each cheese layer. Sprinkle the tomatoes with dried oregano. Fold each tortilla in half.

❖ Brush melted butter over an outside half of each folded tortilla and place buttered side down in a grill pan. Grill with the lid open for 2 to 3 minutes or until nicely browned. Brush melted butter over the top side of each flip. Turn over the flips and grill for 2 to 3 minutes longer or until nicely browned.

❖ Serves 2.

Ham, Brie, and Apple Flips   **Grilled**

Brie and apples are a classic combination. Of all the flips I make, this is my favorite.

> **Prepared honey mustard**
> **2 (8- to 10-inch) flour tortillas**
> **6 thin slices deli ham**
> **6 slices Brie cheese**
> **6 thin slices Granny Smith apple**
> **3 tablespoons melted butter**

❖ Heat the grill to medium-low, about 325 degrees.

❖ Spread honey mustard over half of one side of each tortilla. Layer half the ham, half the Brie cheese and half the apple slices over the honey mustard layer. Fold the tortillas in half, and brush the tops with melted butter.

❖ Place the flips buttered side down in a grill pan, and grill with the lid open for 2 to 3 minutes or until nicely browned. Brush melted butter over the top side of each flip. Turn over the flips and grill for 2 to 3 minutes longer or until nicely browned.

❖ Serves 2.

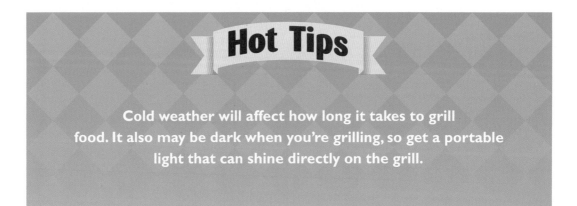

Hot Tips

Cold weather will affect how long it takes to grill food. It also may be dark when you're grilling, so get a portable light that can shine directly on the grill.

Turkey Reuben Flips **Grilled**

If you don't like sauerkraut, these flips would be delicious with coleslaw instead.

> **Thousand Island dressing**
> **2 (8- to 10-inch) flour tortillas**
> **6 slices deli turkey**
> **2 cups shredded Swiss cheese**
> **1 cup sauerkraut**
> **3 tablespoons melted butter**

❖ Heat the grill to medium-low, about 325 degrees.

❖ Spread Thousand Island dressing over half of each tortilla. Layer 3 turkey slices, half the Swiss cheese and half the sauerkraut over the Thousand Island dressing layer. Fold over the top halves of the tortillas and brush with melted butter.

❖ Place the flips buttered side down in a grill pan, and grill with the lid open for 2 to 3 minutes or until nicely browned. Brush melted butter over the top side of each flip. Turn over the flips and grill for 2 to 3 minutes longer or until nicely browned.

❖ Serves 2.

Vegetables
and Side Dishe

Lots of vegetables are great prepared on the grill. Just brush them with olive oil, sprinkle with salt, and cook until they're lightly charred and full of smoky flavor.

My goal in this chapter was to make everything easy to prepare on the grill. Then I hit a road block—how do you make loaded mashed potatoes on a grill? Or pasta salad? Then it hit me—barbecues aren't barbecues without side dishes and not all can be grilled. So this chapter includes some tasty grilled items that you'll find easy and fun to prepare, but it also includes stove- or oven-prepared dishes that are just good matches with grilled food.

Grilled Asparagus **Grilled**

You can use a thicker asparagus, but you'll have to peel it first or it'll be tough. Since I don't know many moms with time to peel asparagus, I'd just put this recipe aside until you can find the pencil-thin variety.

1 pound pencil-thin asparagus
1 tablespoon extra-virgin olive oil
Salt and pepper to taste

❖ Heat the grill to medium-high, about 400 degrees.

❖ Wash the asparagus and trim about an inch from the bottom of the stems. Place the asparagus and olive oil in a medium bowl; toss to coat. Season with salt and pepper.

❖ Place the asparagus in a grilling basket. Grill with the lid open until the asparagus begins to char, turning occasionally with tongs. This takes only a few minutes, so watch the asparagus carefully!

❖ Serves 4.

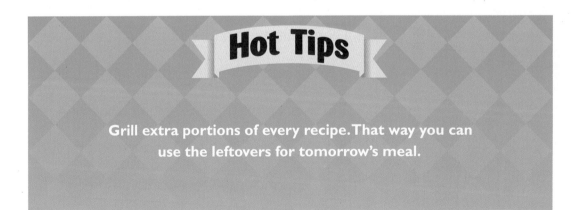

Hot Tips

Grill extra portions of every recipe. That way you can use the leftovers for tomorrow's meal.

Grilled Portobello Mushrooms

Nothing could be simpler than these Portobello mushrooms. Good ingredients prepared simply is the key.

6 portobello mushroom caps
Extra-virgin olive oil
Salt, pepper and dried oregano to taste

❖ Heat the grill to medium-high, about 400 degrees.

❖ Trim any woody stems off the mushrooms and remove the gills by scraping gently with a teaspoon. Brush all sides of the mushrooms with olive oil. Sprinkle the inside of each mushroom cap with salt, pepper and dried oregano.

❖ Grill for 2 minutes. Turn over the mushrooms and grill for 2 minutes longer or until tender.

❖ Note: This is one of those items you throw on the grill when you're already cooking other things. If the grill is heated to medium or high, the recipe will still work. Don't sweat the small stuff.

❖ Serves 6.

Stuffed Portobello Mushrooms  Grilled

You can use any kind of cheese for these mushrooms, but I like buttery fontina because it melts beautifully. Mix your leftover Alfredo sauce with macaroni and a little grated Parmesan cheese for a terrific version of macaroni and cheese.

4 portobello mushroom caps
Extra-virgin olive oil
Prepared Alfredo sauce
1 cup shredded fontina cheese
1 teaspoon dried oregano

❖ Heat the grill to low, about 300 degrees.

❖ Scrape the gills from the mushrooms and remove the stems if they are attached. Brush the outside of the mushroom caps with olive oil.

❖ Spoon about 2 teaspoons of Alfredo sauce into the hollow of each mushroom cap. Top with fontina cheese and sprinkle with oregano.

❖ Place the mushrooms in a grill basket. Grill, covered, for about 5 minutes or until the cheese is melted and the caps are browned.

❖ Serves 4.

Marinated Grilled Vegetables

If you don't like the vegetables I've listed, feel free to substitute your favorites.

2 medium zucchini
2 medium yellow squash
1 medium red, yellow or orange bell pepper
1 small onion
1 sprig fresh rosemary
½ cup extra-virgin olive oil
1 tablespoon balsamic vinegar
1 teaspoon Worcestershire sauce
Salt and pepper to taste

❖ Cut the ends off the zucchini and yellow squash. Cut each vegetable in half lengthwise and then in half again lengthwise (or just make the chunks the way you like them). Core and seed the bell pepper; cut it into chunks. Slice the onion into thick rings and separate. Place the vegetables and the rosemary sprig in a plastic food container.

❖ Whisk the olive oil, vinegar and Worcestershire sauce together in a small bowl. Season with salt and pepper. Pour the vinegar mixture over the vegetables in the container and seal with the lid. Shake the container to coat all the vegetables. Allow the vegetables to marinate at room temperature for several hours, shaking the container occasionally.

❖ Heat the grill to medium-high, about 400 degrees.

❖ Remove the vegetables from the container with tongs and place them on the grill. Grill each side until nicely charred.

❖ Serves 4.

Corn on the Cob

I have seen many recipes for grilled corn on the cob and I have to tell you I don't think they work. Or at least I should say they've never worked for me. The highest and best use of your microwave is for doing corn on the cob. The added advantage of this method is that there's no cleanup, and if you're really cheap, you can use the paper towels for something else. This method was taught to me by Earl Tywater, the late, great owner of Earl's Fruit Stand in Franklin, Tennessee.

4 ears of your favorite corn
Butter (optional)

❖ Wrap each ear of corn in a paper towel. Microwave on high for 3 to 4 minutes or until cooked but not mushy. (Larger ears will require more cooking time.)

❖ Serves 4.

Hot Tips

Dice up leftover grilled red peppers (or yellow or green) and onions. Use them in what we call "crazy" eggs—scrambled eggs with peppers, onions, and grated Cheddar cheese.

Corn and Cheddar-Stuffed Chiles

This is a healthy version of the chile rellenos (or stuffed peppers) so popular in Mexican restaurants. Instead of deep-frying the chiles, this version uses the grill. Chiles vary in hotness, and if your kids don't like spicy food, the cubanelle variety works really well. This recipe calls for a gas grill. If you're using a charcoal grill, just grill the peppers on the cooler part of the grate.

⅓ **cup pine nuts**

  4 **cubanelle or poblano chile peppers**

  1 **(11-ounce) can white Shoe Peg corn, drained**

2 **tablespoons lime juice**

❖ Heat the grill to medium-high, about 400 degrees.

❖ Toast the pine nuts in a skillet over medium heat on the stove (or grill) for about 10 minutes or until they begin to brown, stirring occasionally. Remove from heat. Let stand until cool.

❖ Grill the chile peppers with the lid open until the outside skin is completely blackened. Place the peppers in a paper bag and close the bag to let them steam for about 10 minutes.

❖ Reduce the heat on one side of the grill to medium. Turn off the other side of the grill.

❖ Remove the peppers from the bag and peel off the blackened skin. Make a slit lengthwise in each pepper and remove the seeds and veins.

❖ Place the corn in a medium bowl. Add the lime juice, Cheddar cheese, shallot, cilantro and pine nuts; mix well.

❖ Stuff the peppers with the corn mixture. (The peppers will probably be lying flat. Don't worry about trying to close them.) Spray a grill pan with nonstick cooking spray and place the peppers in the pan.

❖ Place the grill pan on the unheated side of the grill; grill the peppers for about 10 minutes until they are heated through and the cheese is melted.

❖ Serves 4.

Corn Dip Leftover

Stuffed chiles are really good, but what may be even better is what you can do with the leftover corn filling. In certain parts of the South, corn dip is a big hit at summer barbecue parties when the Silver Queen corn is at its height of flavor. I'm begging you to try this it's so good! The quantity this makes depends on how much leftover filling you have.

> **Leftover corn filling**
> **(see Corn and Cheddar-Stuffed Chiles, page 147)**
> **Mayonnaise**

❖ Mix the corn filling with enough mayonnaise to bind the mixture in a bowl. Chill and serve with wheat crackers such as Wheat Thins®.

❖ Yields about 2 cups.

Hot Tips

Use leftover grilled vegetables to make an omelet with goat or feta cheese or cook pasta and stir in the vegetables.

Potatoes with Bacon and Cheese

The trick to grilling potatoes is to cut them in small enough pieces so they cook evenly. The best part is that you can cook the potatoes in a foil pouch. Serve them from the pouch and throw the pouch away! This recipe uses a gas grill. If you're using a charcoal grill, just put the potato packets on the cooler part of the grate. Note: Moms, baking in the oven is the SINGLE best way to cook bacon ever. The bacon always comes out perfectly cooked and there are no grease spatters. The best part is you just throw away the foil when you're done.

1 pound red or Yukon Gold potatoes	**Salt and pepper to taste**
3 tablespoons butter	**1 cup shredded Cheddar cheese**
	3 slices bacon

❖ Heat one side of the grill to medium, about 350 degrees.

❖ Cut potatoes into ½-inch cubes (roughly—this is not a science project).

❖ Cut a piece of heavy-duty foil large enough to form an airtight pouch that will comfortably hold the potatoes. Spray the foil with nonstick cooking spray. Place the potatoes on the foil, dot with butter and season with salt and pepper. Fold the tops and sides of the foil to form a pouch and seal the seams to prevent steam from escaping.

❖ Place the pouch on the unlit side of the grill and grill for about 15 minutes. Pick up the pouch with insulated gloves and shake it to redistribute the potatoes so the bottoms won't burn. Grill for 15 minutes longer; check with a fork for tenderness.

❖ Heat the oven to 400 degrees. Place 3 bacon slices on a baking sheet lined with heavy-duty foil. Bake for about 20 minutes, checking after 15 minutes for doneness. Crumble the bacon after it cools.

❖ When the potatoes are done, open the pouch and sprinkle with the shredded cheese and crumbled bacon. Close the pouch and grill for 5 minutes longer to melt the cheese.

❖ Serves 4.

Pineapple Salsa

Pineapple salsa is meant to be the best supporting actor for Ginger Lime Marinated Tuna (see page 111). You can buy fresh pineapple rings in the produce section of your supermarket, so don't feel as though you have to attack a whole pineapple to make this salsa. You can also use this salsa with grilled chicken or pork. If your little ones can't stand the heat, leave out the jalapeño pepper. And after you cut a jalapeño, don't rub your eyes until you've washed your hands!

> **1 cup chopped fresh pineapple**
> **1 tablespoon chopped fresh cilantro**
> **1 tablespoon minced red onion**
> **1 chopped fresh jalapeño pepper**
> **1½ teaspoons lime juice**
> **¼ teaspoon salt**

❖ Combine the pineapple, cilantro, red onion, jalapeño pepper, lime juice and salt in a medium bowl and mix well. Chill, covered, for about 30 minutes before serving.

❖ Yields about 1 cup.

Tomato and Eggplant Salad

I'll admit that eggplant isn't for everyone, especially kids. If you don't like eggplant, just move along to the next recipe.

1 medium eggplant
3 medium tomatoes
Salt and pepper to taste
Extra-virgin olive oil
1 ball fresh mozzarella cheese
Balsamic vinegar

❖ Heat the grill to medium-high, about 400 degrees.

❖ Cut off the ends of the eggplant and remove the outer skin with a paring knife. Cut into 1/2-inch slices and sprinkle with salt. Drain the eggplant in a colander for about 30 minutes to remove the bitterness.

❖ Cut the tomatoes into 1/2-inch slices. Sprinkle the tomatoes with salt and pepper; sprinkle the eggplant slices with pepper. Brush the tomatoes and eggplant liberally with olive oil.

❖ Place the tomato and eggplant slices in a grill basket. Place the basket on the grill for about 3 minutes with the grill lid closed. Remove the tomatoes. Turn over the eggplant and continue grilling for 4 minutes longer or until nicely browned.

❖ Cut the mozzarella cheese into 1/4-inch slices. Layer half the eggplant slices, half the tomato slices and half the mozzarella slices on a plate. Continue layering with the remaining eggplant, tomato and mozzarella cheese. Drizzle with additional olive oil and balsamic vinegar.

❖ Serves 4.

Stuffed Tomatoes with Goat Cheese

I know, I know. Your kids don't eat goat cheese. As a substitute, if you mix ¹/₂ cup of shredded Cheddar cheese in the stuffing before you add it to the tomato, it's good. But you adults should try the goat cheese. It's really good.

> **4 large ripe tomatoes**
> **I small sweet onion (such as Vidalia), chopped**
> **2 tablespoons extra-virgin olive oil**
> **I cup seasoned breadcrumbs**
> **I small log goat cheese**
> **Nonstick cooking spray**

❖ Cut the tops off the tomatoes, remove the seeds, and carefully scoop out the pulp, making sure the tomato shell stays intact. Chop the tomato pulp and spoon it into a medium bowl.

❖ Sauté the onion in the olive oil in a sauté pan over medium-high heat on the stove until onion is translucent. Add the onion and breadcrumbs to the tomato pulp and stir to combine. Spoon the onion mixture into the tomato shells and top each with I thin round of goat cheese.

❖ Heat half the grill to medium, about 350 degrees.

❖ Place the tomatoes in a grill pan that has been sprayed with nonstick cooking spray. Place the pan on the unheated side of the grill. Grill with the lid closed for 5 to 10 minutes or until the tomatoes are tender and the goat cheese begins to melt.

❖ Serves 4.

Grilled Polenta · Grilled

A roll of prepared polenta is usually found in the refrigerated section of the produce department. Grilled polenta is easy and delicious. Serve it with homemade or store-bought tomato sauce for a light meal, or use it as an accompaniment to grilled pork loin or pork chops.

1 roll of prepared polenta
Extra-virgin olive oil
Salt and pepper to taste
Nonstick cooking spray

❖ Heat the grill to medium, about 350 degrees.

❖ Cut the polenta into 1-inch slices. Brush with olive oil and season with salt and pepper.

❖ Place the polenta slices in a grill basket that has been sprayed with nonstick cooking spray. Grill with the lid closed for approximately 10 minutes or until nicely browned. Turn over the slices with a spatula and grill for 10 minutes longer or until nicely browned.

❖ Serves 4.

Hot Tips

Setting the alarm on a probe thermometer is as easy as setting an alarm clock. Set it for the ideal internal temperature (165 degrees for chicken, for example). When the alarm goes off, the meat is done.

Pesto Red Pepper Pasta Salad

This recipe makes enough for a family of four. It's easy to double the recipe if you're cooking for a crowd. I use penne pasta in this recipe, but you can use any pasta shape you like.

½ pound penne rigate pasta
¼ cup pine nuts
½ cup mayonnaise
¼ cup sour cream
¼ cup prepared pesto
½ cup chopped red bell pepper
¼ cup chopped red onion

❖ Cook the pasta in boiling water on the stove using the package instructions; drain. Place in a bowl and set aside.

❖ Toast the pine nuts in a small skillet over low heat on the stove until they begin to brown. Remove from heat and set aside.

❖ Combine the mayonnaise, sour cream and pesto in a bowl and mix well. Add the pesto mixture to the pasta. Stir in the pine nuts, bell pepper and red onion. Chill, covered, until serving time.

❖ Serves 4.

Tortellini Salad

This makes a very simple salad. If you like your pasta salads with a little more dressing, bottled Italian would work well.

I (20-ounce) package fresh tortellini
½ cup extra-virgin olive oil
2 tablespoons red wine vinegar
I small orange bell pepper, seeded and chopped
I (2-ounce) can sliced ripe olives
I pint grape or cherry tomatoes
I (8-ounce) ball fresh mozzarella cheese, cubed
2 tablespoons dried oregano
2 teaspoons salt
½ teaspoon black pepper

❖ Prepare the tortellini on the stove using the package directions; drain. Place the tortellini in a large bowl. Stir in the olive oil and vinegar while the tortellini are still warm. Let stand at room temperature until cool.

❖ Add the bell pepper, olives, tomatoes, mozzarella cheese, oregano, salt and pepper; mix well. Serve at room temperature if possible.

❖ Serves 4.

Potato Salad with Capers and Dill

Before you look askance at capers in a potato salad, try them. Capers are the small berries of a Mediterranean bush, and they sort of resemble a salty pickle in taste. During my son's Cub Scout days, we would have potluck suppers, and the potato salad with capers was the first thing to be consumed.

6 cups cubed red or Yukon Gold potatoes
1 teaspoon salt
1 cup chopped celery
½ cup chopped red onion
1½ tablespoons capers, drained
1 tablespoon fresh chopped dill
**   (or 1½ teaspoons dried dill)**
1 cup mayonnaise
¼ cup coarse-ground mustard
Salt and pepper to taste

❖ Combine the potatoes with enough water to cover in a saucepan on the stove. Bring to a boil and add the salt. Boil until the potatoes are tender when pierced with a fork; drain. Let stand in a large bowl until cool.

❖ Combine the celery, red onion, capers, dill, mayonnaise and mustard in a medium bowl and mix well. Add the mayonnaise mixture to the potatoes and toss to combine. Season with salt and pepper. Chill, covered, for about 30 minutes before serving.

❖ Serves 4 to 6.

Rice-a-Roni® Salad

This recipe works with any variety of Rice-a-Roni®. The fried rice version has almonds in it, so if your little ones are allergic to or dislike nuts, just switch to another type of Rice-a-Roni®.

> **1 package Rice-a-Roni® Fried Rice**
> **⅓ cup thinly sliced green onions**
> **⅓ cup diced carrot**
> **⅓ cup sliced green olives**
> **⅓ cup plus 1 tablespoon mayonnaise**
> **2 tablespoons sour cream**

❖ Prepare Rice-a-Roni® on the stove using the package directions. Place in a large bowl and let stand until completely cool.

❖ Combine the green onions, carrot, olives, mayonnaise and sour cream in a small bowl and mix well. Add the sour cream mixture to the Rice-a-Roni® and mix well.

❖ Chill, covered, for at least 1 hour before serving.

❖ Serves 4 to 6.

Look for silicone basting brushes in your housewares store. You can just pop them into the dishwasher.

Cucumber and Onion Salad

Japanese cucumbers don't have the high seed content that regular cucumbers have, and their peels aren't waxed, so you can use the entire cucumber.

2 large Japanese cucumbers, thinly sliced
1 medium sweet onion (such as a Vidalia), thinly sliced
1 cup apple cider vinegar
¼ cup vegetable oil
¾ cup sugar
1 teaspoon celery seed
Salt and pepper to taste

❖ Place the cucumbers and onions in a large bowl.

❖ Place the vinegar, vegetable oil, sugar, celery seed, salt and pepper in a small bowl and whisk to combine. Add enough vinegar mixture to the cucumber mixture to lightly coat the cucumbers; toss to coat.

❖ Chill, covered, for at least 1 hour before serving.

❖ Serves 4 to 6.

Rustic Bread ⟩ **Grilled** ⟨

Rustic breads are those loaves with a crunchy crust found at all bakeries and most supermarkets these days. Buy them whole so you can control the thickness of the slices. This recipe is simple, simple, simple, because with really good bread you don't need much else. Give the kids a treat by putting a slice of their favorite cheese on the bread after you turn it over. Close the lid and grill for about 30 seconds to a minute to melt the cheese—instant open-faced grilled cheese sandwiches!

> **1 loaf rosemary olive oil rustic bread**
> **(or any other kind you prefer)**
> **Extra-virgin olive oil**
> **Salt to taste**

❖ Heat the grill to medium, about 350 degrees.

❖ Slice the loaf into 1-inch-thick slices. Brush both sides of the bread slices liberally with olive oil and sprinkle with salt.

❖ Grill the bread slices for 2 to 3 minutes or until the grilled side has deep brown grill marks. Turn over the slices and grill the other side until it also has deep brown grill marks.

❖ Yields 8 or more slices.

Cheesy Garlic Bread

Fontina cheese has a creamy, nutty taste and is well worth seeking out in the specialty cheese section of your grocery store. If you can't find it, good old mozzarella will work just fine. This recipe is for a gas grill. If you're using a charcoal grill, place the bread on the coolest part of the grate and watch it carefully so it doesn't burn.

> **1 loaf French bread**
> **Extra-virgin olive oil**
> **Fontina cheese**
> **Dried oregano**
> **Garlic salt**

❖ Heat one side of the grill to medium, about 350 degrees.

❖ Split the loaf of bread lengthwise and brush liberally with olive oil. Slice the fontina into thick slices and layer it over the cut sides of the bread. Sprinkle with oregano and garlic salt to taste.

❖ Place the bread with the cheese side up on the unheated side of the grill. Grill with the lid closed until the cheese is melted and the bread is crispy, beginning to check after 5 minutes.

❖ Serves 4.

Sour Cream Smashed Potatoes

The skin stays on the potatoes for this recipe, meaning the most nutritious part of the spud will find its way into your kids' stomachs. If you've never made homemade mashed potatoes, you'll find they're worth the effort. Don't worry about getting all the lumps out—these potatoes are meant to be smashed, not silky smooth. A potato masher is a simple device, but it's the best one for the job—if you don't have one, invest in one.

> **1 pound baby fingerling or red potatoes,**
>   **cut into chunks**
> **1 ½ teaspoons salt**
> **¼ cup (½ stick) butter**
> **¼ cup milk**
> **2 heaping tablespoons sour cream**
>   **Salt and pepper to taste**

❖ Combine the potatoes with enough water to cover in a large pan on the stove. Bring to a boil and add the salt. Boil until potatoes are tender when pierced with a fork; drain.

❖ Return the potatoes to the pan to dry for a minute. Add the butter and the milk. Mash the potatoes with a potato masher until they are smooth with just a few lumps remaining. Stir in the sour cream, salt and pepper.

❖ Serves 4 to 6.

Loaded Mashed Potatoes

This is my version of a loaded baked potato. These potatoes go really well with the Grilled Meatloaf (see page 84)—comfort food at its finest.

**1 pound red or fingerling potatoes,
cut into quarters or other equal-sized pieces**

1 ½ teaspoons salt

¼ cup (½ stick) butter

¼ to ½ cup milk

½ cup shredded Cheddar cheese

¼ cup sour cream

2 tablespoons snipped fresh chives

2 slices bacon, crisp-cooked, crumbled

½ teaspoon salt

❖ Combine the potatoes with enough water to cover in a large saucepan. Bring to a boil and add the 1½ teaspoons salt. Boil until potatoes are tender when pierced with a fork; drain.

❖ Return the potatoes to the pan to dry for a minute. Add the butter. Mash the potatoes with a potato masher. Add the milk slowly, mashing until the potatoes are the consistency you like.

❖ Add the Cheddar cheese, sour cream, chives, bacon and the ½ teaspoon salt. Mix well with a spoon.

❖ Serves 4 to 6.

Roasted Potatoes and Carrots

Nothing is easier than roasting potatoes and carrots. I've made this recipe a thousand times, and the best part is there's no cleanup—when you're done you just throw away the foil lining the pan. This method also works with any kind of hard squash, turnips, or parsnips.

> **1 pound fingerling or small red potatoes**
> **½ pound baby carrots**
> **Extra-virgin olive oil**
> **Salt and pepper to taste**

❖ Heat the oven to 400 degrees.

❖ Wash the potatoes and cut them into quarters. If the baby carrots are thick, cut them in half lengthwise.

❖ Arrange the potatoes and carrots over a foil-lined baking sheet. Drizzle olive oil over the potatoes and the carrots and mix well so that every piece is coated. Season with salt and pepper.

❖ Roast the potatoes and carrots for 10 minutes. Stir with a spoon and roast for 10 minutes longer or until potatoes are tender and browned.

❖ Serves 4 to 6.

Orange Rice with Pine Nuts

Orange juice gives this rice dish a lush flavor that goes particularly well with grilled chicken breasts.

¼ cup pine nuts
1 cup chicken broth
¾ cup orange juice
1 cup long-grain white rice
¼ cup chopped dried cherries

❖ Toast the pine nuts in a saucepan over low heat on the stove. Remove from heat and set aside.

❖ Combine the chicken broth and orange juice in a saucepan and bring to a boil. Stir in the rice; return to a boil. Reduce heat and simmer, covered, for 15 to 20 minutes. Stir in the pine nuts and cherries.

❖ Serves 4.

Hot Tips

Nonstick cooking spray fixes almost everything. For almost all recipes, lubricate the grill with nonstick cooking spray before adding the food.

Couscous with Mushrooms

Couscous is the easiest thing in the world to cook. Just boil water, add these tiny grains of pasta, cover the pot, and remove from the heat. Wait 5 minutes and it's done. You can add all kinds of extras to the pot. At my house, sautéed mushrooms and Parmesan cheese are favorites.

> **1 tablespoon butter**
> **1 cup sliced button mushrooms**
> **Salt and pepper to taste**
> **1 cup water**
> **¼ teaspoon salt**
> **1 cup couscous**
> **4 tablespoons butter**
> **½ cup grated Parmesan cheese**

❖ Melt the 1 tablespoon butter in a sauté pan over medium heat on the stove. Sauté the mushrooms in the butter for 10 minutes or until nicely browned. Season with salt and pepper.

❖ Pour the water into a 1-quart saucepan and bring to a boil. Add the ¼ teaspoon salt and the couscous. Remove from heat and let stand, covered, for 5 minutes. Fluff the couscous with a fork. Add the mushrooms, the 4 tablespoons butter and the Parmesan cheese; mix well.

❖ Serves 4.

Janis's Baked Beans

It's a miracle that my friend, Janis Faircloth, came up with this recipe, because she doesn't cook. Her daughter, Lindsey, grew up eating frozen dinners and begging a home-cooked meal from the neighbors. Janis served this dish at our annual "Girls' Beach Weekend" and everyone loved it.

½ pound ground chuck
½ cup chopped onion
⅓ cup sugar
⅓ cup firmly packed brown sugar
½ cup barbecue sauce of your choice
¼ cup ketchup
½ teaspoon salt
½ teaspoon pepper

½ teaspoon chili powder

❖ Heat the oven to 350 degrees.
❖ Brown the ground chuck with the onion in a large sauté pan over medium-high heat on the stove, stirring until crumbly; drain.
❖ Combine the ground chuck mixture, sugar, brown sugar, barbecue sauce, ketchup, salt, pepper, chili powder, molasses, Dijon mustard, kidney beans, butter beans, pork and beans and bacon in a large bowl and mix well. Spoon the bean mixture into a buttered 2½-quart baking dish. Bake, uncovered, for 1 hour.
❖ Serves 8 generously.

Green Bean and Corn Casserole

Okay, so this is not a diet dish. But it's really tasty. If you don't want to bake the entire dish at once, prepare the whole recipe and freeze half of it.

> 1 can cream of mushroom soup
> 1 cup sour cream
> 1 ½ cups crushed butter crackers (such as Ritz®)
> 2 (14-ounce) cans French-style green beans, drained
> 1 (14-ounce) can Shoe Peg corn, drained
> 1 (8-ounce) can sliced water chestnuts, drained
> 1 small onion, chopped
> 1 cup shredded sharp Cheddar cheese
> 1 ½ cups crushed buttery crackers
> ½ cup (1 stick) butter, melted

❖ Heat the oven to 350 degrees.

❖ Combine the condensed soup and sour cream in a medium bowl and mix well.

❖ Line a 9×13-inch baking dish with 1 ½ cups crushed buttery crackers. Layer the green beans, corn, water chestnuts and onion over the crackers. Layer the soup mixture, Cheddar cheese and the remaining 1 ½ cups crushed buttery crackers evenly over the onion mixture. Drizzle the melted butter over the top.

❖ Bake for 30 to 35 minutes or until brown and bubbly.

❖ Serves 8.

Cheesy Cornbread Complement

Heating the shortening in the oven before adding the batter gives the cornbread a nice brown crust.

> **¼ cup solid shortening (such as Crisco®)**
> **1 (6-ounce) package cornbread mix**
> **1 (8-ounce) can creamed corn**
> **1 cup shredded Cheddar cheese**

❖ Heat the oven to 450 degrees.

❖ Coat the inside of a 9x9-inch metal baking pan with the shortening and heat the pan in the oven for about 15 minutes.

❖ Prepare the cornbread batter in a bowl using the directions on the package. Stir in the creamed corn and Cheddar cheese.

❖ Remove the baking pan from the oven and pour in the cornbread batter. Return the pan to the oven and bake for about 20 minutes or until a wooden toothpick inserted in the center comes out clean.

❖ Serves 4 to 6.

Cornbread Salad

You don't see this "salad" very much outside the Deep South, but it's a delicious way to use up leftover cornbread. If you don't have leftover cornbread, well, it's worth making a fresh batch just for this salad.

4 cups (at least) crumbled leftover cornbread
2 (15-ounce) cans kidney beans, drained
1 large tomato, chopped
½ cup chopped red onion
½ cup chopped yellow bell pepper
2 cups shredded Cheddar cheese
8 slices bacon, crisp-cooked, crumbled
2 cups bottled ranch salad dressing

❖ Spread half the crumbled cornbread in the bottom of a 2-quart baking dish. Layer half the beans, half the tomato, half the onion, half the bell pepper, half the Cheddar cheese and half the bacon over the cornbread. Drizzle half the salad dressing over the top. Layer the remaining cornbread, beans, tomato, onion, bell pepper, cheese and bacon over the salad dressing layer. Drizzle the remaining salad dressing over the top.

❖ Chill, covered, for at least 1 hour before serving.

❖ Serves 6 to 8.

Desserts

I wish I had received the "baking" gene when I was born, but I did not. I have tried my hand at pies and cakes, and I take my hat off to those cooks who can turn out a tender crust and a tasty cake from scratch. So my desserts tend to be the kinds of things that don't require a lot of science.

Some of my desserts are made on the grill, but most are not. There are some things a grill was not meant to do.

Grilled Fruit Kabobs  Grilled

You may substitute other fruits for the pineapple or strawberries, such as peaches or plums. Fresh pineapple is available year-round in the produce section of most grocery stores.

1 container fresh pineapple chunks
1 pint strawberries
½ cup (1 stick) butter, melted
Granulated sugar
Prepared chocolate sauce

❖ Heat the grill to medium-low, about 325 degrees.

❖ Remove the strawberry tops and cut the strawberries in half. Spear the pineapple chunks and the strawberries alternately on metal skewers or bamboo skewers that have been soaked in water for 30 minutes.

❖ Brush the melted butter over the skewered fruit. Sprinkle with the sugar.

❖ Grill the fruit kabobs with the grill lid up, turning the fruit until each side is slightly charred.

❖ Serve with chocolate sauce for dipping.

❖ Serves 4.

Grilled Mixed Fruit ➤ **Grilled**

You can use this fruit as a topping for ice cream, angel food cake, or pound cake.

4 tablespoons butter
2 Granny Smith apples, peeled, cored, sliced
2 Bartlett pears, peeled, cored, sliced
1 cup raisins
½ cup sugar
1 tablespoon cinnamon

❖ Heat the grill to medium-low, about 325 degrees.

❖ Melt the butter in a saucepan. Add the apples, pears and raisins; stir until the fruit is coated with butter.

❖ Mix the sugar and cinnamon together in small bowl.

❖ Tear off 4 squares of heavy-duty aluminum foil large enough to fold into packets. Place ¼ of the fruit mixture over each square of foil. Sprinkle with the cinnamon mixture. Fold each aluminum square into a packet, enclosing the fruit mixture and sealing very tightly to keep juices from leaking.

❖ Arrange the packets on the grill. Grill with the lid closed for about 5 minutes or until fruit is tender when tested with a fork. If fruit is not tender, reseal the packet and grill for a few minutes longer.

❖ Serves 4.

Cinnamon Sugar Pound Cake **Grilled**

Prepare the whole recipe, or just grill a couple of slices for the kids.

¹/₂ cup sugar
1 tablespoon cinnamon
1 prepared pound cake
   Butter, softened
   Vanilla ice cream
   Prepared strawberry ice cream topping

❖ Heat the grill to medium, about 350 degrees.

❖ Mix the sugar and cinnamon together. Cut the pound cake into 1-inch slices. Spread one side of each slice with butter and sprinkle with the cinnamon sugar.

❖ Arrange the slices on the grill sugared side down. Butter and sugar the other side. Grill with the lid up for about 2 minutes or until the cake begins to brown. Turn over the slices and grill the other side.

❖ Top the grilled cake slices with ice cream and strawberry topping.

❖ Serves 6 to 8.

Apple Cheese ⟩Complement⟨

This has been a recipe in our family for years. It may have had a better name at some point, but that has been lost in the mists of time. You wouldn't think these ingredients work together, but they do.

1 (21-ounce) can apple pie filling
½ cup (1 stick) butter, softened
1 cup sugar
¾ cup flour
8 ounces Velveeta® cheese

❖ Heat the oven to 325 degrees.
❖ Pour the pie filling into a 9×9-inch baking pan. Combine the butter, sugar, flour and Velveeta® in a medium bowl and mix until blended. Pat the Velveeta® mixture evenly over the pie filling.
❖ Bake, uncovered, for 30 minutes.
❖ Serves 4 to 6.

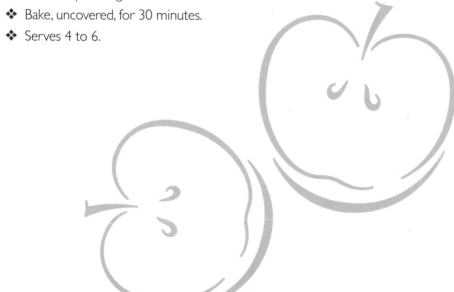

Blueberry Cobbler

This cobbler can be made with fresh blackberries during blackberry season, or with frozen blueberries if fresh ones are unavailable.

4 cups fresh blueberries
4 tablespoons sugar
1 tablespoon cornstarch
1/2 teaspoon fresh lemon juice
1 cup all-purpose flour
2 teaspoons baking powder
1/2 teaspoon salt
1/2 cup whole milk
1/3 cup butter, melted
1 egg, beaten

❖ Heat the oven to 375 degrees.

❖ Spread the blueberries in an ungreased 2-quart baking dish. Sprinkle with the sugar, cornstarch and lemon juice and stir until gently mixed.

❖ Combine the flour, baking powder and salt in a medium bowl. Add the milk, butter and egg; stir just until the batter is blended.

❖ Pat the batter over the blueberry layer. Sprinkle with additional sugar if desired.

❖ Bake for 30 to 35 minutes or until the crust is nicely browned.

❖ Serves 4 to 6.

Vanilla Cream Dried Fruit Pie

This recipe comes from my good friend Terrell Jones, a buddy of mine on the barbecue circuit. Terrell is about 80 years young, and he remembers his grandmother making this pie, which is his favorite and mine, too. Terrell's original recipe includes a meringue topping made from 3 stiffly beaten egg whites and 6 tablespoons of sugar. I omitted that part because at our house, we're not big on meringue.

1 (5-ounce) package dried apples	2 cups milk
1 cup apple juice	1/3 cup sifted flour
1/2 cup water	2/3 cup sugar
1 tablespoon sugar	1/4 teaspoon salt
1/2 teaspoon cinnamon	3 egg yolks, lightly beaten
1/4 teaspoon nutmeg	2 tablespoons butter, melted
1/4 teaspoon salt	1/2 teaspoon vanilla
	1 baked (9-inch) pie shell

❖ Heat the oven to 350 degrees.

❖ Combine the dried apples, apple juice and water in a medium saucepan over medium heat on the stove. Stir in the 1 tablespoon sugar, cinnamon, nutmeg and 1/4 teaspoon salt. Cook, stirring occasionally, for about 20 minutes or until the apples are tender. Remove from heat.

❖ Microwave the milk in a glass dish just until warm. Combine the flour, the 2/3 cup sugar and the remaining 1/4 teaspoon salt in a 2-quart saucepan over low heat on the stove. Add the warm milk gradually to the flour mixture and cook until thickened, whisking constantly. Remove from heat. Whisk a small amount of the hot milk mixture into the egg yolks in a bowl. Return the yolk mixture to the hot milk mixture and mix well. Stir in the butter and vanilla. Cool completely.

❖ Spread the apple mixture in the bottom of the piecrust. Top with the vanilla cream.

❖ Bake for 12 to 15 minutes.

❖ Serves 8.

Faux Bananas Foster

Real Bananas Foster means adding a banana liqueur to the pan and setting it on fire—not a good idea in a house full of kids and kind of scary for adults, too! This version tastes just as good and doesn't involve a call to the fire department.

> 1/4 cup (1/2 stick) unsalted butter
> 1 cup firmly packed dark brown sugar
> 1/3 cup pulp-free orange juice
> 1/4 teaspoon cinnamon
> 4 bananas
>   Vanilla ice cream

❖ Melt the butter in a heavy sauté pan over medium heat on the stove. Add the brown sugar. Cook over low heat until the brown sugar is dissolved, stirring constantly. Stir in the orange juice and cinnamon.

❖ Peel the bananas and halve them lengthwise. Add them to the brown sugar mixture, stirring to coat the banana pieces. Cook the banana mixture for about 5 minutes or until bananas begin to turn tender.

❖ Serve the banana mixture over ice cream in individual bowls.

❖ Serves 4.

S'more Sandwiches ▶ **Grilled**

This is my version of the classic campfire treat.

8 slices cinnamon swirl bread
Marshmallow fluff
Peanut butter
Milk chocolate chips
Butter, softened

❖ Heat the grill to medium, about 350 degrees.

❖ Spread 4 slices of bread with marshmallow fluff. Spread the other 4 slices with peanut butter. Sprinkle chocolate chips over the peanut butter and close the sandwiches.

❖ Butter one side of each sandwich. Arrange the sandwiches on the grill, buttered side down. Butter the other side of each sandwich.

❖ Grill with the lid closed for about 2 minutes. Turn over the sandwiches. Close the lid and grill until the bread is nicely browned.

❖ Serves 4.

Peanutty Ice Cream Sandwiches

I love peanut butter cookies, and that's why I choose them for this recipe. But you can make these homemade ice cream sandwiches with any kind of store-bought cookie dough and any kind of ice cream. Let your kids pick their favorite combinations. I use the cookie dough that makes extra-large cookies.

> **1 roll refrigerator peanut butter cookie dough**
> **Granulated sugar**
> **1 pint butter toffee ice cream, softened**
> **½ cup crushed peanuts**

❖ Cut the cookie dough into ¼-inch slices and coat each slice in granulated sugar. Bake the cookies in the oven using the package directions. Remove to a wire rack to cool completely.

❖ Spread one spoonful of ice cream over a cookie. Top with a second cookie to make a sandwich. Repeat the process with the remaining cookies.

❖ Roll the ice cream edges of the cookie sandwiches in the crushed peanuts. Freeze for at least 10 minutes before serving to let the ice cream harden.

❖ Yields 6 ice cream sandwiches.

Hot Tips

We have a rule in our house: She who cooks doesn't clean up. This rule is especially satisfying after you've made something really messy.

Parfaits with Tortilla Sugar Crisps

The tortilla sugar crisps are so good you may want to skip the rest of the recipe and eat them all by themselves. If you're not up for whipping your own cream, you can substitute a whipped topping.

1/2 cup sugar
1 tablespoon cinnamon
4 flour tortillas
Vegetable oil
2 cups heavy cream
1/4 cup confectioners' sugar
1 pint strawberries
1 pint blueberries

❖ Combine the 1/2 cup sugar and cinnamon in a small bowl.

❖ Cut the tortillas into wedges. Heat about 1/2 inch of oil in a heavy skillet over medium-high heat on the stove, until it is hot enough that a tortilla wedge slipped into the oil will begin to brown.

❖ Fry the tortilla wedges for 15 seconds or until lightly browned. Drain the wedges on paper towels and sprinkle with the cinnamon sugar.

❖ Whip the cream with an electric hand mixer until stiff peaks form. Add the confectioners' sugar gradually, beating constantly at high speed.

❖ Cut the strawberries into halves or fourths depending on their size. Layer the strawberries, blueberries and whipped cream in alternating layers in a parfait glass or other clear glass. Garnish with the tortilla wedges.

❖ Serves 4.

Notes

Catherine Mayhew is wife to Mark, mother to Noah, and a life-long enthusiastic cook. She is a former restaurant critic for the *Charlotte Observer* and syndicated food columnist for the Knight-Ridder Wire. She lives in Brentwood, Tennessee, where her deck is home to five grills. When she's not grilling, she's competing with her all-female competition barbeque team, Chicks in Charge.

Photograph by: Noah Chapin Mayhew

Catherine Mayhew